What Others Are Saying…

Beautifully written with dramatic prose and insights, Army Chaplain's wife Robyn Graham has penned a remarkable book, sure to touch the lives and hearts of many readers. Whether or not you have personally experienced the debilitating effects of childhood abuse, you will be heartened by the strength of Robyn's faith and fortitude during her years of recovery. This book will serve to provide essential understanding of a darkened world that so many children experience in today's society. Robyn's compelling and stirring story will help all of us to understand better how to encourage and uplift the broken hearts and fractured spirits of far too many young people affected by abuse. Robyn takes us on her journey to find peace and forgiveness and hope for living. A loving wife and mother of three, she has demonstrated what the love of Christ and caring people can do to repair the brokenness of an abused childhood. I admire Robyn's transparency and her courage to share this remarkable story with us.

Dr. Larry N. Chamberlain, President and CEO,
Grace Brethren Investment Foundation, Inc.

Robyn Graham has bravely opened her life, all of it. She allows the reader to walk with her down a path of blunt honesty as she shares her early life filled with pain, abuse, and mental and emotional suffering. We are reminded that, for all too many of our youth, their life is reflected in Robyn's experience. The refreshing quality of her book is that she has tenaciously held on to her faith in her Lord, even from her early days. Somehow, she was able to bear the pain, heal the wounds, find forgiveness, and turn her scars into a means of reaching out to others who have had to walk a similar pathway. Today she serves alongside her Army chaplain husband with tenderness, passion, and commitment that have grown out of her journey. Her life is reflected in her wonderful children, her ministry presence to military wives, children, youth, and to all with whom she comes in contact. I highly recommend her openly written memoir, especially for all who long to have the love of Christ reflected in their lives and who have a desire to reach out to troubled people on their life's journey.

Dr. John W. Schumacher, FGBC Endorsing Agent,
CH (COL) USA, Ret.

When I first heard Robyn and Billy speak at a marriage conference in Korea, I immediately knew we were 'kindred spirits'. After reading Robyn's story, it was confirmed. Through the grace of God she had overcome horrendous obstacles in her life. I too had similar experiences and was reminded of the grace and mercy of God in my own life. Even when we feel alone, as if no one knows what we are going through and that no one cares, God is with us. After reading Robyn's life story, I was encouraged and reminded that we are all overcomers through Christ Jesus! I believe this story, written straight from Robyn's heart, will bless and encourage others who may feel defeated and alone.

Stacey Reynolds, military wife,
mother of four (two adopted), and 4th grade teacher

Honest, poignant, and disturbing, Robyn Graham's book *He Touched Me* has something to say to everyone, regardless of gender, economic status, or religion. She writes of the unspeakable, and in doing so, she reaches out to the hearts of those who have struggled silently and sometimes not so silently with burdens too hard to bear alone. Robyn writes with a strong sense of faith in God that has come through intense struggle. Her voice is strong and clear—God is faithful. We can count on Him.

Patricia Nichols, US Army chaplain, chaplain's wife,
and mother of four boys.

This is a well-written and powerful book. I cried when I read what Robyn had to endure in her childhood. But she shows how God's power can be triumphant in all circumstances. She helped me understand what children of child abuse are feeling and the effects it can have later on. As a parent of an adopted older child who had to endure a difficult early childhood, I found it Robyn's story to be very helpful. I thank her for being so honest and willing to tell her story.

Sandy Wood, wife of a colonel in the US Army,
mother of four children, one adopted from Korea.

As the mother of an adopted daughter, who has gone through trauma in her young life, *He Touched Me* gave me some insight into how her little mind might be thinking…and how she deals with the pain of past memories. I believe [this] story will be a ray of hope and an inspiration to others who are suffering the horrors of child abuse. How thankful I am to have read it.

Leanne Allison, wife of a US Army colonel,
mother of two children, one of whom is adopted from Korea

[He Touched Me is] a compelling story of the courage and perseverance of a young girl overcoming years of abuse and the faithfulness and steadfastness of our mighty God whose hand leads her from the darkness into the light of His love, mercy, and grace.

Sheri Lewis, post librarian,
wife of a division chaplain, and mother of two

[Robyn's] book is gripping. It is truly a journey into her private hell and torture field as a child. She doesn't leave you there, however…Her writing is brutally honest, but comes from the heart of …a caring individual who consistently demonstrates in her words and actions that God was still there for her every step of the way…She has become an awesome woman for God despite overwhelming personal obstacles.

Gail Lee is a military wife and homeschool mother of four.
Her experience, like Robyn's, testifies to the amazing Grace of God
who pulled her through a dysfunctional family life to Himself.

He Touched Me

A Memoir

The story of
a life that was
touched by many.
Sometimes lovingly.
More often than
not, painfully.
But never as deeply
as when touched by
the hand of God.

He Touched Me

A Memoir
by
Robyn Graham

BMH Custom Books
www.bmhbooks.com
Winona Lake, IN 46590

He Touched Me
A Memoir

Copyright ©2008 by Robyn Graham

ISBN: 978-0-88469-093-1
RELIGION / Christian Life / Personal Growth

Unless otherwise noted, Scripture quotations are from
The Holy Bible New Living Translation, copyright ©1996.
Used by permission of Tyndale House Publishers, Wheaton,
Illinois 60189. All Rights Reserved.

Published by BMH Custom Books
BMH Books, P.O. Box 544, Winona Lake, IN 46590 USA
www.bmhbooks.com

Printed in the United States of America

Dedication

This book is lovingly dedicated to:

My Dad ~ Melvin Dykstra
Whose unselfish love and encouragement showed me the way
to my Heavenly Father and whose hugs never cease to heal.

My Mom ~ Phyllis Dykstra
Who smiled and laughed while numbering her sermons
and who patiently continues to show me the difference
between boundaries and cages.

My Husband ~ Billy Graham
Who is constantly, compassionately trying to coach me out of
my cages and incredibly understands when I lock myself back in.

My Children ~ Katie, Joy, and Christopher
Who have become three of the most amazing people
I know and who constantly challenge me to look at
things in new and exciting ways.

Special Thanks

I am so thankful to God for Larry Chamberlain, president of the Grace Brethren Investment Foundation, and his vision for getting my story into the hands of people who may be helped and encouraged by it. The sponsorship of this book by GBIF goes beyond anything I could have asked or imagined.

Larry's work with the Eagle Commission, supporting and encouraging Grace Brethren Chaplains is heartfelt and genuine and has been such a blessing to our family. The Eagle Commission has supported us through two deployments, including our current ministry in Korea! I don't know how we are to repay Larry and the Eagle Commission for all the help and encouragement they are to us.

My husband Billy spoke recently on "Paying it Forward," and I think that is the only way to honor the Eagle Commission and what they mean to us. The help and encouragement we receive we pay forward by helping and encouraging the soldiers and their families wherever we are. The personal and financial support that Larry, his wife Sherlene, and the Eagle Commission have given to the publishing of my story is something entirely too big for me even to begin to pay back or pay forward. I'm asking God to help Larry and the Eagle Commission to know how truly thankful the GrahamCrackers are to have their support.

Robyn

Contents

Preface

A while back, my duplex neighbor and I sat talking about how horrible military life can get. As both our husbands were gone on their second deployment, we had a lot to commiserate about. Between the two of us and our six kids we've had to deal with broken and sprained bones, almost every one of the appliances breaking down, and we've even had the fire department show up on two occasions. We've done holidays and birthdays, anniversaries, and all school events on our own. And we've spent countless hours waiting for the weekly 10-minute crackly phone call to come. As we sat that day, wallowing in each other's misery, I told her I was writing a book that I was going to title, "Life Sucks!" She laughed, but my kids were in shock! "Mom! Only the really bad kids in school say that word!" Oops. My bad!

We have always been language-conscious in the Graham household. We never use the words "hate" or "stupid" and would absolutely never tell anyone to shut up. "Angry words" my kids call them, are still not allowed in our home but since the kids have started public school they've learned a whole new vocabulary! I'm finding that there are new slang and swear words for every generation. I tried to explain to my kids that when I was in school the word "suck" and all its many forms was the accepted slang of the day. Everything "sucked." By the look on their faces, I could tell they weren't buying it. My oldest daughter, a well-taught home-schooler, said, "Let's look it up!" So we did.

Sucks—*vulgar slang—to be disgustingly disagreeable or offensive.* Okay. Round one goes to the kids. Although it's very true that life can be disgustingly disagreeable, I didn't want to be accused of being vulgar, so I began looking for a better title. I thought about "Life Stinks," but you know, life doesn't just stink. Stink is a pair of smelly socks or sour milk. Life can be much worse than that. So I gave up the search for the perfect title and began writing.

When I was done, I sat back and began to think about what this book is really about. More than whining about military life—although I'm sure some of those experiences will appear on the following pages—this is a book about my past. Writing about my life was my chance to stand behind the two-way mirror and point my timid, shaking finger at the person in the lineup and say, "That's the one." "He raped me." "She beat me." "He left me." "She disowned me." "He touched me."

That was just the beginning though. Publishing this narrative was like having to go to the courtroom and point out my attackers in front of the world. No safety glass, no two-way mirror. Face-to-face in front of a room of judging people who may or may not believe me, who may or may not be on my side. Some will encourage, and some will question everything I say, causing doubt and panic, belittling and berating me until I'm the abused little girl backing up into her cage once again. Regardless of the outcome, I have been able to say out loud that I was neglected, raped, and abused. It was a huge first step but it was only a step—a giant step along the path of healing that has taken years and will continue to take years. It has been, and continues to be, a journey. As one friend put it, "A journey from being a victim to being a survivor." It's a journey I wanted to share with others so they could know that someone else has been there. I want those who are hurting to know there is hope and healing. I so want them to be able to look back as I have done and see the good and know that there is a loving God who can and will bring beauty from pain.

There are two other things that have made it difficult for me to finish this monumental task of writing my life's story. One is that every time I read through what I've written I question, "Is it too much?" "Is it not enough?" One friend who had done some publishing and editing work read through a bit of my story, and what I deduced from her comments was: Don't leave the reader hanging. Don't leave them at the bedroom door wondering what happened behind it. People are tough. They're hardened by the media and the world around them and they almost anticipate the gory details, as it were.

The problem is that there are times I don't even know myself what went on behind some of those doors. I'm still working on my "junk" as you'll see in this narrative. It has really been a struggle for me to know how much of the gory details to write out. Sometimes I think that if I spell out my abuse, moment by moment, maybe it will empower others to do the same with the abusive situations they have gone through. It hurts my heart to think of those who keep their abuse to themselves, thinking there is safety in the fact that nobody else knows about it. It hurts my heart when I hear from people who have lived with the entire burden of the abuse because they think no one else will believe them if they told the truth. I want others to be empowered to acknowledge that they were abused as well as to have some hope of recovery and healing.

My other thought in not wanting to share every abuse and every detail, is that so many people have their own bedroom doors. I can take them to that point and they know, or are just remembering, what went on behind their own closed doors. People know what's crammed in their own bedroom closets and in the oozing boxes under their beds. I thought, perhaps, that it wasn't necessary for my details to be known as long as I could get across the point that there is help and healing on the other side of abuse.

The other difficulty for me was that I wanted to be able to tell my story without causing pain to those whom it affects: my father and mother, my brothers and sisters, the people who were placed in charge of me. There are so many people this narrative affects. I have no desire to cause them pain. I have a friend who didn't deal with her father's sexual abuse until later in life. When she finally faced this ugly circumstance in her life, she chose not only to confront her father, but to prosecute him. It has ruined his life. He was fired from his job, lost his standing in his community, family and friends have deserted him.

Maybe you are thinking, "Good! Serves him right! He ruined her life, it's only right that his gets ruined!" Yes, I get that. I've been there, but I am not there anymore. I was fine with pointing out and writing about the abuses that took place in my life. I felt relatively safe behind the two-way mirror, thinking I can see them,

I can point them out, I can acknowledge what they did to cause me pain. It was still very difficult, but safe in a way. I didn't want to "go to court," so to speak, and publicly prosecute these people. That wasn't my intent in writing this book. Please don't get me wrong. This is not a feel-good, "lovey dovey," "forgive and forget" kind of book. Some people deserve and need to be prosecuted for their actions. The thief on the cross was still a thief and although Jesus forgave him while he hung there, he still hung there. He still paid the consequences for his actions. I just do not want this story to help some and hurt others, although I realize that cannot be helped. I don't purposely want to bring pain to those who have been a part of this narrative and that alone has made it incredibly difficult to make the decision to finish and publish this book.

~†~

A preface, I'm told by my oldest daughter who reads voraciously, is to state what the author's purpose is in writing the book. Although I may have had many personal goals as I worked through and wrote of the pain and abuse I suffered in my life, my main goal in publishing this book is to bring hope to those who have had similar experiences. I want them to know that someone else has been there. It has taken me so long to do so because I have struggled with balancing how many details to share and what to withhold; all the while conscious of the fact that the people I am writing about will perhaps read this some day and their lives will be affected as well. My prayer is that I have, with God's help, achieved that balance and that what is written in the following pages will only bring hope and the promise of healing to those who are hurting.

One more thing: I am not attempting to give a perfectly accurate view of history, just an incomplete but heartfelt view of a few moments of my life. These are my memories. They may differ from yours. No two people see or remember things exactly the same. I have changed or rearranged some of the names, but if you recognize yourself among these pages, please know that I do not say the things I do to be hurtful. Please also know that if you are one of the people who have caused me pain, I have, with God's help, forgiven you. You will hopefully see that I have only striven to use the pain in my life to grow. I am in the process of ridding my heart and mind of the bitterness and resentment caused by the circumstances you may have been a part of. Forgive me for any pain this narrative may cause you. Also, please forgive me for any pain I may have brought to your life as our life's journey found us along the same path at times. I hope that through my words you will be able to find help and healing as I have, and perhaps God will allow our paths to cross once again under much pleasanter circumstances. If not, I pray that we will meet in heaven where the only One who has the power to heal and forgive will wipe all our tears away and we will be free to know His love and to give His love in full.

Introduction

Beauty from Pain

When bedtime came at the small house on Wilbur Street, five children were sent upstairs without ceremony. "You have five minutes to get into your pajamas and into bed. I better not hear one sound after that, or else...." There were no bedtime stories. No lullabies. No goodnight hugs and kisses. I'd heard of such things in stories and from friends but I didn't really believe they existed. Two of my sisters and I quickly changed into our pajamas and climbed into bed. We had triple bunk beds that at times were stacked up so high there was barely room for me to slide into my covers without knocking my head into the ceiling. We'd also had the beds spread out separately in the tiny room but in this memory they were all pushed together making one big bed and I was sleeping closest to the door.

I said five children went up the stairs but there were seven children in the house. The two babies were in the room across the hall. They were still too small to put themselves to bed and had already been asleep long before we were sent upstairs. I wonder if they got lullabies and goodnight kisses and it's just something we'd outgrown. Two babies in one room, my two sisters and I in the second, and that leaves my two brothers in the room next door, the room that was connected to our room by a long closet. It's this closet that I dreaded. Not the closet itself, exactly, but I dreaded the fact that the closet door was open and I dreaded knowing who may and probably would come through it. Although I would have loved to close the closet door, I knew that if my stepmother heard my feet on the floor I would be in for it. I was still bruised from the last beating, so I turned my head away from the closet door, put my hands underneath my pillow, grasped the wooden spindles of the headboard and fell off to sleep. Suddenly I was jerked wide-awake as I was pulled from my bed to the floor by my brother.

The rest is just a part of the recurring nightmare that I knew I would never be able to tell a soul about. Who would believe me? And besides I knew he'd make my life a worse hell than it already was if I ever told anyone. So I kept my eyes closed and pretended to be asleep in another world. A world where there are no men with staring eyes and wandering hands, no curious, nasty boys, no teachers with beards and Jeeps, and no wicked stepmothers.

~†~

It's been nearly thirty years since I lived in that house on Wilbur Street and I still sleep with my hands beneath my pillow, searching for something to grab onto. I cannot go to sleep at all if the closet door is open, in fact I keep my closet so crammed full of clothes and junk that no one could ever get through. I've kept my heart and mind that way as well—crammed full of rubbish, oozing out of closets and seeping out from under the bed. I am tired of the stench. Even more so, I am tired of living in fear. So I've decided to deal with the yuck.

You've been there. You have your own skeletons in the closet. You have your own memories stored away in boxes where you think they will be out of sight, out of mind. But they never really are. We never really forget. Our hearts won't let us forget. Even the most painful events come back to us in flashes of panic and dread. I know so many people who have been abused in some way, or in many different ways, in their life and have spent years with the entire weight of the abuse on themselves. They keep the memories locked up and hidden away, having never told a single soul. What a tremendous burden. I know. I have done the same.

There are things written in this book that I have never told another living being. Not even God. And now I'm telling them to you. Why? I started writing for selfish reasons, actually. I wanted to get the yuck out of my mind and I thought if I put it on paper, I could put it away from me. Then as I wrote of the abuse and neglect in my life, I realized I needed something more. My mind was full of memories and my heart was full of questions, the biggest one being "why?" Why did this happen? Why didn't someone stop it? Why did God allow it? Although I rarely got answers to those questions, just being able to ask them was a huge beginning. Now, here I am, sharing my thoughts and memories with you, not wanting to burden you with my yuck but hoping and praying that this narrative will empower you to deal with the "stuff" you've packed away in your own boxes and closets and under beds.

I know that sometimes it may seem like this current pain is all we'll ever know. How often have you wondered if your life would ever be "normal"? Have you sat in anxious fear dreading the next panic attack or flashback? Have you cried out to God wondering when your past would stop haunting your every moment? You are not alone. There are millions and millions of us in this world who endure pain or the memory of pain almost every day of our lives. Our past sucked! But it was the past. I encourage you to look back. Stop hiding, stop pretending, and stop carrying the weight of your past all by yourself. Please, I want to encourage you, if you're going to look back, only do it to find the good. Don't hang on to the pain. Don't seek after revenge. Don't let those who hurt you in the past continue to hurt you now. I wish I could help you. I wish I could hold your hand or bring you the box of tissues or help you yell at God or whoever it is you're angry at. I'd like to be the person behind the two-way mirror with you, as I feel like you are being for me, and give you a safe place to point out your abuser and say out loud "He touched me," "She beat me," "He raped me," "She abandoned me."

The best I can do for you is to tell you I've been there. I know God loves you. I know He was with you at every moment and I am able to say to you without a doubt that my God has never let me down. I know that He works ALL things for good and it is my hope and prayer that you will know His touch and that someday He will bring beauty from pain.

The lights go out all around me
One last candle to keep out the night
And then the darkness surrounds me
I know I'm alive, but I feel like I've died

And all that's left is to accept that it's over
My dreams ran like sand through the fist that I made
I try to keep warm but I just grow colder
I feel like I'm slipping away

My whole world is the pain inside of me
The best I can do is just get through the day
When life before is only a memory
I wonder why God let me walk through this place

And though I can't understand why this happened
I know that I will when I look back someday
and see how You've brought beauty from ashes
and made me as gold purified through these flames

Here I am at the end of me
Trying to hold to what I can't see
I forgot how to hope, this night's been so long
I cling to your promise that there will be a dawn

After all this has passed, I still will remain
After I've cried my last, there'll be beauty from pain
Though it won't be today, someday I'll hope again
And there'll be beauty from pain

Chapter 1

Jesus Loves the Little Children

The slate-gray house stood apart from the others in the neighborhood for only one reason. It didn't look any different from any other house in this scary "ghetto" part of town. The paint was peeling and chipping away off the rotting boards. The cinderblocks that held up the house were cracked with a few corners broken away, just like most of the other houses. The roof leaked, the windows were cracked, and the screen door was ripped in two places. The front yard, what there was of it, was strewn with cans, toys, and a lonely discarded shoe.

What made this house different was that it was occupied by monsters, not people. Wild Things lived inside. They were children once, perhaps they still are under the layers of dirt and grime and beneath the hard exterior they have developed to survive. Inside the house, they have piled all the furniture in the middle of the room and are jumping from couch to chair to couch to end table. One creature bumps into another and the fight begins. The yelling and screaming brings one of the monsters, my little sister, in from the kitchen where she was rummaging through fridge and cupboard and garbage can looking for food. The pursued, me, and the pursuer, my brother, ran into a bedroom and in less than a second blood curdling screams issue from the room and reverberate off the walls of the house. Little did we know that the wildest of all the wild things, my oldest brother, was lying in wait on the top bunk of the bunk beds. As soon as we entered the room he threw his weapon, which was a hammer, and it hit its mark, which was me, on the side of the head and I went down bleeding and screaming.

"Where were your parents?" you may well ask. "Wasn't there any adult supervision?" Good question. You would know if the adults were home only by the slight change in scenery. The wild things became caged, neglected animals when our parents were there.

~†~

"Rusty, I'm hungry," I whispered to my older brother. "Me, me! I want bottle," my three-year-old sister, Dee, added quite loudly. She was still learning to put her words together in an order that made sense and what three-year-old knows what it means to whisper? It was late at night and we girls had not eaten yet that day. "I know, Dee!" said our brother, Rusty. "Be quiet would ya? I can't sneak downstairs with you making all that noise!" Dee began to cry and I put my arm around her as our other brother, Randy, said, "Go on Rusty. I'll stay and keep them quiet. Where's Mom and Dad?" Randy was only six years old, but he tried to sound as tough and brave as he could. His young voice still came out sounding a little worried. "I don't know." Rusty, who never sounded worried, growled, "I think they're out on the porch. I'll be fine." And with that the seven-year-old crept downstairs in search of food and drink while the other three waited quietly in the desolate upstairs bedroom.

The room was indeed desolate. It was completely empty of color or comfort. No pictures adorned the walls; no furniture hugged the corners of the room, inviting the idea of rest or care. The only thing in the small bedroom was an old rolled up bit of smelly carpet in the middle of the cold, brown linoleum floor. This is where the four of us children spent the majority of our time, when our parents were home. Set among the dingy walls and cracked ceiling, the carpet served as whatever furniture we needed at that particular moment: a couch, a bed, and hopefully soon, a table to eat at. The bedroom was situated at the top of a rickety set of stairs covered in a nasty brown carpet. The stairs were one of two sets in the house. This one went up to the second story bedrooms; the other went down to a cold, creepy cement basement that housed the wringer washing machine and little else. The house was an old brick duplex that sat near the corner of Hall St. just across from the elementary school. The road was paved with old bricks, and the old houses that lined the streets were close enough together that you could shake hands with your neighbor as you hung out your window. There was, however, more shooting than handshaking going on among neighbors in this part of town.

Rusty was the oldest of the four of us kids and he was quite adept at sneaking. He made it to the kitchen without a sound. He had two cans of food in one arm and was filling up a second baby bottle with sugar and water when he heard our parents' voices from the porch start to rise in anger. He quickly screwed the top on the second bottle and had just reached the bottom step when he heard the front door slam. "I hate you!" came the angry voice echoing up the stairs behind him. "You're gone all the time! You leave me here with those monsters you call children! Why did you even want me to have kids? You're not here to help me take care of them! I'm sick of them! I'm sick of you! I hate this life! I want a divorce!" These words were spoken by our mother who was a young woman of about twenty-six years of age. Not too young to be responsible for children and a household but too miserable to be responsible. She was a very unhappy young woman indeed and unwilling in her unhappiness to look past herself to the needs of her young children. The last word she screamed, "divorce," echoed and bounced off the bare bedroom walls as Randy shut the door behind his brother, Rusty, who was already dumping his load onto the nasty floor.

"What's dee force?" I asked. My eyes were as big as saucers and rimming with tears.

"Oh, who cares?" came Rusty's answer. "It just means no more yelling cuz Mom and Dad won't live together anymore! Do you want beans or corn?" This was the best answer Rusty could give as he handed us girls each our own baby bottle. "Come on Goob, beans or corn?" (I was nicknamed Goober after the peanut butter and jelly swirled together in a jar; it was my favorite thing to eat) I couldn't answer. I sat with tears streaming down my cheeks. As the reality of the situation sank in, I said, almost in a whisper that began growing into a panicked cry, "Dad will leave? Dad will go away? Dad won't be here anymore!" Smack! Rusty's hand flew through the air, landing across my face, leaving a bright stinging red mark behind. "Shut up, would ya, and eat!" No one else said a word. Rusty pulled the can opener from his back pocket and we opened our cans and ate our dinner in silence.

Angry voices wormed their way between the cracks in the walls and under the doorway. Words were punctuated with breaking glass and slamming doors. It wasn't what you would consider silence, but we kids were silent nonetheless. When the cans were empty, though our stomachs were far from full, Dee and I curled up with our sugar-water baby bottles and put our heads on the carpet like a pillow. Rusty and Randy curled up on the filthy floor, their shirts rolled up as their pillows and a frightened, saddened four-year-old little girl began very softly to sing the song I had learned at the church our neighbor had taken us to just a few days before…"Jesus loves the little children, all the children of the world. Red and yellow, black and white, they are precious in His sight. Jesus loves the little children of the world."

~†~

These are some of my earliest memories. There are many snapshots similar to these. There are nearly a dozen houses, empty but for spare furniture, growling stomachs and angry voices. I have these mini memories but I really have no clear idea where I was or who I was with during that early time of my life.

Although I may not always have known who I was living with, I know who was with me. God. I think as children we are somehow born with a great amount of faith. Kids have an innate sense of what is good and right and beautiful in this world...they still seem fresh from God. Yes, even two-year-olds! They will still climb into your lap, look right into your eyes and remind you that God smells like the rain.

It's not hard for me to look back on my early years and be able to picture myself climbing up into my heavenly Father's lap in the midst of a storm and still be able to smell the rain. I must've still known in my heart there was a God who made the world and who loved me. I'm sorry to say that it doesn't take long for the world to knock one about enough that beautiful thoughts and precious faith are soon lost.

Chapter 2

"All I Need to Know…"

Robert Fulghum has written a book titled: *All I Really Need to Know I Learned in Kindergarten.*[*] If that is true, I'm in trouble! I know from school records that I attended three different schools in kindergarten. I must've learned something while doing all of that moving around. I remember learning to read. I spent a lot of time coloring pictures of giant hamburgers and cutting out pictures from magazines. I had my first boyfriends in kindergarten! (Don't tell my girls. They're fifteen and sixteen years old and they're not allowed to even think about having a boyfriend!) Anyway, I say boyfriends not because I had several but because they were twins…Mick and Nick O'Pattrick. Aren't their names great? We would hold hands during the little "movies" and they would bring in pencils or wild flowers and leave them on my desk. What do you actually learn in kindergarten? I guess I should read the book because I don't know that what I learned in the kindergarten classroom is all that important. I do know I learned

*Robert Fulghum, *All I Really Need to Know I Learned in Kindergarten* (New York: Ballentine Books, Rev. Ed., 2004).

a lot more about life than I did about ABCs and 123s during that year.

The first kindergarten teacher I remember was very tall and very handsome, at least to a five-year-old! He had a beard and mustache; he looked a lot like my dad actually (minus the beer belly) and he had a Jeep! We had a long ugly red station wagon at home and I always thought it would be so awesome to have a Jeep. The thought of the open roof and the windows down, the wind blowing in my hair and face—just everything about a Jeep fascinated me. It was my dream car.

Well, this teacher would on occasion pick a few students to come to his house on the weekend to swim in his pool. One Friday I got a note saying I was chosen to be among the few to go to his house that weekend. I was so excited. This is the first memory I have of being genuinely thrilled about something. I was always the one to sit quiet in the background unnoticed. Like Mia Thermopolis said in the movie *Princess Diaries*, "I am invisible and I'm good at it." This was the first time someone noticed me and picked me out to do something special. The house I was living in at the time was the brick duplex on Hall Street that I described earlier. I remember waiting by the street sign until my teacher came to pick me up. I could see the school playground from where I stood. This playground is where I remember getting my tongue frozen to one of the metal bars and the police and the fire department had to come and help pry it off. Yes, I actually stuck my tongue to a metal pole like the kid on "A Christmas Story." I was standing outside waiting for my teacher to come and was so excited that I was dancing and singing to myself like only a five-year-old can do.

There were already two of my classmates in the Jeep when the teacher pulled up in front of my house. I hopped in and let me tell you, this was the best part of that day. The ride in the Jeep was everything I had imagined it would be, except that I didn't get to sit in the front seat. The wind was in my hair and on my face, blowing away all memories of the anger and noise of home. I was free. I was special. For a moment. Only for a moment, for of course I could not have realized what "special" plans he had in mind for me and perhaps the others. I still don't remember the details of the rest of that day. I can only remember the ride in the Jeep and the long white hallway leading down to the white bedroom door. Maybe someday I will remember the rest and be able to deal with my fear of closed doors and men with beards.

~†~

The other kindergarten I remember is the one I attended and graduated from while in a foster home. During my stay at this home I learned how to ride a bike, I had my first boyfriends, (Mick and Nick O'Pattrick), I learned how to read and to write my name, I even had a kindergarten graduation (I still remember the blue velvet diploma). It was in this foster home that I began to realize what it means to be "abused."

Go back with me one more time to the house on Hall Street. Remember the big fight my mom and dad were having? Well, sometime during that night, the fighting at the brick house escalated until neighbors called the police and protective services. I had remembered the fighting and the strange people who came to put all of us kids into a big van but it was late and dark and I fell asleep on the long ride. When I woke up sometime in the dark of the early morning I found myself in a strange place. Surrounded by strange smells and strange beds and strange nighttime noises, I called out as loud as I dared for something familiar. "Where are we?" My small voice whispered through the dark. "Randy? Are you there?" "I'm here" came his whispered answer, "we're all here but not Rusty. They took Rusty somewhere else." "Where are we?" I asked again as I reached my hands through the bars of what I could now recognize as a crib. It was a cold metal crib and my sister Dee was in the crib next to mine. As I tried to reach the hand of my sleeping baby sister, my brother Randy tried to explain about the people who came in the night and brought us to this place because our mom and dad had been fighting so awfully. He promised that everything would all be okay. "Just go back to sleep. Don't wake up Dee whatever you do!"

Morning light came and with it came a warm bath, clean clothes, and pancakes and scrambled eggs. The nurse who bathed and dressed us girls wore a constant warm gentle smile on her face. She talked in almost a whisper as she asked us questions about whether we went to school and what we liked to play. She took Dee and me by the hand and led us down a long hallway to a room filled with tables and chairs. Kids were all sitting down eating or standing in line getting a plate of hot breakfast. "It's just like kindergarten at lunch time," I thought. "I wonder if there are teachers?" Inwardly, I shuddered at the thought. I've already told you what happened at my last kindergarten, when my teacher took me and two other classmates home to his house to swim, but swimming was not all he had planned. I definitely did not want to think about that now, or ever and besides, warm food and the bath were so wonderful! Only happy thoughts today. I had just begun to wonder where Randy was when I spied him with two other boys at a table already gobbling down a stack of pancakes.

The three of us, Randy, Dee, and I, had been brought to a sort of halfway house, a place for kids to stay while they wait to be adopted or to be placed into a foster home. We would not stay here long for we were going to live with a foster family who lived out in the country about an hour from the halfway house.

We handled this next move better than you might expect. We were used to being moved from home to home, person to person. As I look back, I realize that what I would experience in this new home would prove to be something I had not yet learned to deal with.

Chapter 3

Worth Less

The foster home was set in a small town where everyone knew everyone. You could hold hands in kindergarten and no one thought of suing you for sexual harassment. You could go Trick or Treating, walking the entire town, and not have to check your apples for razor blades afterward. We pretty much lived a normal American life. The house itself was a large two-story dwelling, and the first thing I noticed was the big climbing tree out front. I loved climbing trees and this tree looked like it would do just fine! The other thing I noticed were the cornfields. There were very few buildings to be seen, and the skyscrapers of the city had been replaced with silos and barns. There were two or three other houses on down the street and I wondered if there would be kids to play with. I wondered whether we'd be allowed to play. We were used to coming and going as we pleased with no one really caring where we were or who we were with. One look at this mom and dad and you could tell they meant business. This was going to be the kind of place where there were rules and regulations and where a kid needed to be seen and not heard and to mind their P's and Q's.

The foster parents had three kids of their own. There were two girls who were older than I by a few years, and a little boy who was about my age. We settled into life here as best we could. It was wonderfully different to have three warm meals a day and to all sit down around a table to eat. But it was horribly different to see how they treated their own children compared to how they treated us. I can't say that I expected to be treated like one of the family. I didn't really know what to expect. Still, life was not horrible. Even though they had their own beds and we had to sleep on the floor, we had slept in worse situations. We were used to hard work and being punished. I think what made it so difficult was that we saw, for the first time in our young lives, people in the same house being treated better than we were. It was demeaning and demoralizing and although I would never have used those big words as such a young child, I do remember feeling worth less somehow.

Everything was different here. I was glad Randy and Dee were with me and I often wondered what they thought of things. I wondered if they knew why we were treated so differently. Randy would know but there was never a time to ask him or Dee because we were never left alone. The truth is that I can hardly remember being left alone for one minute, except perhaps when we went to the bathroom or were finishing up a task or cleaning up our room. How is it possible then that I can remember feeling so very alone? It is probably because, even though there were eight people living in the house, no one talked to me. They talked all around me like I didn't exist.

This suited me just fine, most of the time. I really didn't want to be noticed anymore. Mr. K., my new foster dad, noticed me a little too much and one day "noticing" led to another closed bedroom door.

There was a day that I knew it was just he and I in the house. I stayed upstairs as long as possible, making my "floor" bed, straightening my things. When I was done, I headed toward the stairs. I heard my name being called as I reached the top step. Even as I took that first step of the long flight down, I felt the foreboding sickening feeling in the pit of my stomach. "I want you to come here." I reached the bottom step. "In here," he called again and I realized he was calling me from his bedroom that was just around the corner from the stairs.

I went to the door as slowly as I possibly could, trying to convince myself as I went, "It's okay. It'll be fine. It's nothing. He probably wants you to help him with something. Don't worry Robyn." When I got to his door, he told me to stop right there. He was lying in bed. He was dressed from the waist up but the rest of him was covered with a sheet. "Take your clothes off. All of your clothes." When I just stared at him with uncomprehending eyes, he yelled, "NOW!" And I did. And he watched. When I was undressed he had me come to him and "sit on his lap." I tried not to cry as pain shot through my little body. I was so scared and so wanted it to be over that I must've made my mind go someplace else. The next thing I remember is standing in his bathroom quickly washing my face and hands. I had to go back through his bedroom to get to the rest of the house but he was gone, the bed was made, and there was no sign that evil had just taken place.

That night as Mrs. K. helped us get ready for our bath as she always did, she noticed that my underwear was on inside out. She was obsessed with underwear. She would always check to see whether we changed them every day. She would count how many we had in our clothing pile. When she saw that mine were on inside out that night, the look on her face shook me to my inner being. It so looked like she wanted to hit me but she didn't. Did she know what her husband had done? How can you live in a house with someone and not have any clue about these things? Did she ask me why they were on inside out? Even if she did, I'm sure I didn't tell the truth. I didn't tell anyone.

I buried that memory so deep within me that I didn't remember it again until I was an adult going through counseling. I did tell my caseworker about it because I was so upset that they could still be foster parents and still abusing kids! The result? I was told that if I really wanted to pursue this accusation I would have to take a lie detector test and then statements would have to be given and possibly court. That overwhelmed me. It made me feel like they didn't really believe me. It made me start to doubt my own newly discovered memory.

I didn't doubt it long though. I knew what I remembered was real. I knew what had been done to me was wrong but I just decided to stuff it back down inside my mind and not deal with it. It wasn't until just recently that I've been able to take that memory out and look at it long and hard. That has been the biggest step in healing for me. Just being able to say, "Yes, that was real, it did happen. You were a little child and you were scared and alone so you buried the memory" gave me one less bedroom door to fear.

I don't know why this circumstance had to happen in my life. I doubt whether I'll ever know, but I've been able to forgive that man for what he did to me. I've been able to forgive his wife for what I felt she should've known, for what I thought she should've done to prevent it. As I write that, I wonder out loud...how? How did I forgive them? How do I know I've forgiven them? Is it like that sometimes? Can a person just wake up one day and realize, "Hey, I'm not angry about that any more? I don't want to get even. I don't feel anything whatsoever about the situation." Weird. Perhaps it's because it is one of the circumstances in my life that I've allowed to be real and that I've taken to my heavenly Father and asked for His healing. It is the only way I can imagine having my heart and mind clear of the pain that it caused me as such a young child. I felt used and not loved. The truth is I don't remember any loving touches or loving words from this family. I don't remember a hug or a pat on the shoulder or anything. It was like we weren't really people.

I remember coming in from school one day and sitting down at the kitchen counter to finish coloring a picture that I had started in class. The K.'s oldest daughter had come in the kitchen with me and she was having a conversation with her mom about her day at school and having a snack. The girl noticed my coloring.

"Mom, why does she color like that?"

"Like what, dear?"

"Like with all those holes left over? Why doesn't she color hard and fill in all the spaces?"

"I don't know, dear. Perhaps nobody took the time to teach her how to color."

"How long are they going to be here? We share our room, our clothes, our toys, and I want my own stuff for myself."

"I know you do, dear. They won't be here much longer. Their mom and dad are getting a divorce and they don't have anyone to look after them right now. They will soon though, dear. Soon they will go home and you and your sister can have your room back to yourselves. Will that make you happy?"

"Oh, yes. Thank you, Mommy. Can I have another cookie?"

My foster mother gave her oldest daughter another cookie and without having even offered a first cookie to me, she put the rest away and left the room. As soon as she was gone from the room, the older girl began to stare over my shoulder for a few minutes more at the weird coloring, and then she began singing to herself:

"Soon. Soon. You'll be going home soon.

All mine. All mine. My stuff will be all mine.

Robyn, Robyn, go away. Don't come back on a rainy day."

I suppose it was because life was "normal" that I was able to survive this environment. What is normal anyway? Wouldn't it be nice if our lives looked a little like a Norman Rockwell painting? Well, they all do from time to time. Just a little piece of "normal." Moments here and there. We rode the bus to school. We ate dinner around a table. We sat together and colored pictures. We went Trick or Treating. It is amazing how people throw just a second of "normalness" into their world of wickedness and so it fakes the victim into thinking this is what normal life is like; this is how everybody lives, get used to it.

It was God's blessing, in a way, to think that life was normal, because abuse and neglect were a routine part of how I grew up. It was a horrible way to live, but I was powerless to change it and so one of the biggest things God did for me then was to give me the tools I needed to survive. The agency that placed us in the foster home had a motto and still does to this day: "Bloom Where You are Planted." This was God's gift to me. It was His planting a seed, a very small seed deep in my heart. Growth would happen only after I endured years of abuse and neglect. Eventually the little girl inside of me would be nurtured and would grow to know what God promised in 2 Corinthians 4:8 and throughout His Word, and as Sara Groves so beautifully put to music:

> We are pressed but not crushed, Perplexed but don't despair.
> We are persecuted but not abandoned.
> We are no longer slaves.
> We are daughters and sons and when we are weak,
> He is very strong.
> And neither depth nor height, nor present nor future
> Can keep us from the love of Christ!

Chapter 4

A Moment of Hope

Randy, Dee, and I did leave that foster home soon after little Miss K. sang her song at me. We went home to be with our mom and a man who would become our stepfather. All I can tell you about him was that he was a tiny bit of a man with dark skin and a funny accent. He was from Puerto Rico and raised rabbits. I found out the hard way that the rabbits were not pets but food. It was another place, another face, and another adjustment to be made. Somehow, I knew we wouldn't be there long, either.

Remember the little girl curled up by the roll of carpet singing, "Jesus Loves the Little Children..."? Well, there comes a time in our lives when our simple childlike faith starts to change and we look to the world and the people around us for input. I'm thinking of the movie "Short Circuit." I found it on DVD at Wal-Mart the other day in the $5.88 bin. I was so excited! My kids had never seen it and I hadn't seen it in 15 years. The story is about a robot that gets struck by lightning and suddenly becomes "alive." He realizes he has a mind of his own—kind of like a two-year-old—and suddenly is craving input! Like the robot, Johnny 5, we get our input from all kinds of sources: from country preachers to country music, children's books and comic books, and especially TV. We spend a lot of our childhood trying to match what we used to simply believe to what we begin to hear and see.

I began to learn a lot about God at this time in my life, but I certainly wasn't able to match the loving God image to what I saw from the different sets of parents who were dressing me up and either dragging me or sending me with someone else to church to learn about Him. My stepmother was the worst. If I thought I had experienced everything by age seven, boy was I in for a shock. In second grade we were brought home to the definitive "wicked stepmother." Almost immediately after going to live with our mom and stepfather, she started talking about us going to live with our dad and within a week or so we began having "visits" with him and his new wife at their little apartment. The only word I can think of to describe these visits is "scary." Staying at an apartment with two adults for two days doesn't sound like a very scary adventure, does it? Well, that's because you haven't met HER. We had. She was tall, thin, and very beautiful, with thick, wavy brown hair and big brown eyes. She had a big broad smile and an air about her that made you feel like she could do anything for you, if you asked her to. She was like the "White Witch" in *The Lion, The Witch, and The Wardrobe*, and we kids soon found out, as Edmund had, that she could hand out Turkish Delight one minute and dry crusty bread the next. I still remember our first visit.

~†~

The smell was absolutely atrocious. I had heard one of the workers say atrocious at the halfway house and I fell in love with the word. We were about to have our first breakfast with my dad and his new wife at their little apartment. Dinner last night was not atrocious but our behavior must've been. I never knew there were so many rules to eating. Sit up straight. Elbows off the table. ("Honestly! Have these children been taught nothing?!") Twirl the spaghetti in your spoon and bite off what doesn't fit into your mouth. Chew each bite at least twenty-five times and above all, absolutely no slurping. Rules or no rules, I guess I should've known better than to try to eat my spaghetti with my pinky fingers while our heads were bowed for prayer. That dumb move got my hands smacked. This morning French toast was on the menu, which sounded lovely, but the syrup my stepmother poured over my plate was dark molasses syrup that smelled like vomit and dirty socks—atrocious. It really made me nauseous but she wouldn't believe me. I guess throwing up all over the living room floor was not a good way to prove my point and it certainly won't ever make the top ten ways to make friends and influence future stepmothers. Yikes. She was not happy and as I scrubbed up the mess on my hands and knees I was glad that this was just a visit and that I was going back with my mom and stepdad in the morning.

I should have opened my eyes to the reality in front of me. We were going to live with my dad and this new wife of his. It was just a matter of time. In fact, it wasn't long before the following scene took place.

The hot August sun shone down on the small town of Wherever, Michigan, from the brilliant blue afternoon sky above. It was the weekend of my seventh birthday and I, along with my sister and two brothers, was crammed into the back seat of an old green clunker of a car. Our mother was at the wheel and her new husband, our stepfather, sat in the passenger's seat. Between them was the newest addition to the family, their three-month-old little girl, Jules. Although the wind coming through the windows and the noise of the muffler made it plenty loud, we kids were silent with fear. Our mother was driving us across town heading once again for a "visit" with our dad and his new wife. We had already been to two weekend visits with him and "The Witch" at his small apartment and those experiences led us to a state of fear.

Adding to our fear was that we were quite sure this was more than just a weekend visit, mainly because sitting in our laps were paper sacks filled with all of our earthly possessions. Mom had said to bring a few extra things to "play with" during the visit. Well, we only had a few things; namely the few raggedy pieces of clothing we owned and one or two personal things that were special to us.

In Rusty's sack were his baseball and threadbare glove. He loved playing any kind of sport, but baseball was his favorite. Randy, who loved to draw and was always doodling on whatever he could get his hands on, had his pad of drawing paper that his art teacher let him keep along with all his drawings. Dee had her most prized possession with her, but not in her bag. It was a snow globe that she had clutched in her hand while the snow swirled all around the quaint little Christmas scene. In my bag, along with my favorite Sean Cassidy outfit, was the big white family Bible that had all the family names written in the front and the old fancy painted pictures of the various Bible stories and Jesus. I have no idea how I came into possession of it but I loved it dearly. I also had my brown glass piggy bank that had the two quarters I had gotten from Mick and Nick O'Pattrick and a penny that I had found on the street in front of the old house on Hall St.

The car stopped and I remember sitting there a moment, holding in the questions I didn't dare ask. How long are we going to stay? When are you coming back? Do we really have to live with her? Will you come for visits? I really wanted to ask the last question. As cold and heartless as my mother seemed at times, she was really a free spirit. She loved life and enjoyed people and experiences. She loved to laugh. Even though a lot of times the laughter was directed at me, like the time when they cooked my pet rabbit for dinner, I still loved to hear her laugh. I loved her free spirit. I wanted to know I wasn't losing that forever, that I would see her again. I just didn't have enough courage to ask. Besides, no definite answer meant hope and possibilities.

Rusty, Randy, and I piled out of the car and headed up the stairs to what I was sure would become our new home, while our little sister Dee remained hidden in the back seat.

"I know you're back there, Dee! Now go on!" said our frazzled mother as she gave a pacifier to the crying baby in the front seat. "Dee! Go on now, your dad's waiting for you! If I have to get out of this car and yank you out by the hair... so help me..." It was a good thing that I came running back to the car. "Come on Dee Dee! There's cake and everything!"

Slowly, reluctantly Dee gave up and got out of the car. We gave a quick wave to our mother as she threw an "I'll see you soon" out the window and drove off. There. A moment of hope. She said, "I'll see you soon" and even if it was a lie it would be something to hold onto if things got bad here. But for now there was cake and ice cream and the newness of home.

Chapter 5

"Mommie Dearest"

There wasn't anything extraordinary about the house that made it stand apart from the rest of the houses that lined Wilbur Street. It may have been a little bigger or a little smaller than its neighbors and brick instead of wood or aluminum siding, but there was nothing out of the ordinary about the place. There was no caution sign as you turned the corner saying "Evil Ahead." There was no "Slow Down: Abused Children at Play" sign, no tourist signs pointing you to the place where the "Wicked Witch of the West" lived. 3015 Wilbur Street looked like an average small-town home where normal people lived and worked and played. It wasn't, I'm sorry to say.

The two-story brick home stood in a small yard of grass that was overdue for a mowing most of the time. There were no trees in the front yard, but a wild rose bush grew up next to the porch so that the tops of the thorny stems could just be seen peeking their heads over the top of the porch wall and around the sides toward the front of the house. The old red station wagon would rest itself in the gravel driveway; a driveway that led to an old worn-out garage. It was a dilapidated building that was probably only still standing because it couldn't make up its mind which way to fall. Behind the garage was the back yard that was about three times as big as the front yard. There were two trees back there: one small wiry tree (the kind that you can climb to the very top of and sway back and forth); and there was the climbing tree of all climbing trees at the back right corner of the yard against the fence. There was also a clothesline and a small garden plot overgrown with weeds.

Walk up the cracked front steps to the covered porch with me, and we'll travel back in time. Pull up a wooden crate or an empty box. There are no lovely porch swings or rocking chairs in this story. It's 1976 and this normal average brick house is where the four of us kids, Rusty, Randy, Dee, and I spent the next seven years of our lives.

It started the moment we stepped in the door on that hot August day. The first words out of my stepmother's mouth spoken to my sister Dee and me, were something like, "It's about time. Don't you know it's rude to keep people waiting? Take off your shoes at the door. Uhhhhgg! What is that horrible smell? Go straight into the bathroom, both of you and wash those disgusting feet!" "And use plenty of soap," she added as she closed the bathroom door behind us.

Have you seen the movie, "Mommie Dearest"? The wealthy movie actress adopts two children and then proceeds to make their life a living hell. The children were given everything they could possibly need, everything except love. The actress was very temperamental! She would freak out about the smallest things and take it out on the children. One of the girl's chores was to clean the bathroom with gritty cleanser. If "Mommie Dearest" felt any grit at all, she would pour a whole new can of cleanser in the tub and make the child start all over. There were other things like toys and wire hangers that would just set her off and the abuse would begin. Life was good otherwise. They had a beautiful home and beautiful things. They would even have beautiful moments thrown in here and there to make the children think everything was okay, normal, survivable.

My stepmother was just like "Mommie Dearest," and guess whose job it was to clean the tub? Mine. She was not an actress but an aspiring country western singer with her own band. Oftentimes the band would come to the house to practice, which was wonderful in many ways. It entertained us and it kept her mind on other things. She loved her music and even taught us how to sing a couple of songs. Two of them we sang when we went with her to the bars and one she taught us to sing for Sunday morning church. Standing in front of the twenty-five or so people at that little Baptist church singing "You can't be a beacon if your light don't shine…" life was as normal as I ever had it. There's that "normal" word again. What made life normal? I'll look it up.

Normal – adjective – functioning in a natural way; lacking observable abnormalities or deficiencies. Noun – The standard, the usual or expected state or degree.

We sat down at the table at every meal. We brushed our teeth, got dressed and walked ourselves to school every day. We took vitamins and went to church. We went Trick or Treating and Christmas caroling. Life functioned in a normal way with no appearance of abnormality or deficiency. We were clean, well dressed, and well fed. For all intents and purposes, as far as the world could see, our family was normal.

My stepmother was a fantastic cook. I recall cherries jubilee (the stuff you light on fire) one birthday and we had homemade clam chowder every Christmas Eve. She loved to do birthdays and holidays big! She kept us clean, very clean, and well dressed. She taught us how to take care of ourselves physically. Bathing, hair care, teeth brushing—it was all very good for us that we finally had someone to care for us in this way. She wanted us to be the "All American Family," and it was important to her that we at least looked the part, especially at church and during the holidays.

It was the times in between the holidays and birthdays that were awful. My stepmother had a wicked temper and a very low patience level, never a good combination, and she had her hands full. There were four of us from my dad's first marriage. She had a daughter from her first marriage and she and my dad had two children together, totaling seven kids in one house. That's a lot of laundry. If your focus isn't on your home, if your heart isn't attached to those whom you are trying to take care of, there will be nothing but anger and frustration. With my stepmother, there were plenty of both and they were taken out on us. I don't know how to begin to tell you of the abuse that we suffered at this woman's hand.

I remember her missing a red scarf one time. We all had to search the house for hours. Every hour on the hour she would line us up (this was one of her favorite rituals) and one by one we were asked, "Did you find it?" or "Did you do it?" or "Did you take it?" After each of us had answered "No," we would all have to go into her bedroom one by one to be punished. She had a wide variety of belts she would bring out on these occasions. Sometimes she would use a wire hanger, a cutting board or wooden spoon, or whatever was close at hand. But mostly it was belts, and she didn't care which part of our body she would hit.

I also remember my stepmother's jar of canned pickles. I don't know why she was obsessed with those pickles, but she was. She put the jar in the cupboard above the sink and would check that all six pickles were in the jar every day. It was weird. Well, one day there were only five pickles. She flipped out. We stood for hours! It seemed like all day that day, "Did you steal my pickle?" "Did you?" "Did you?" We didn't dare lie. If we were caught in a lie the punishment was Dial soap. Not just your average everyday washing the mouth out with soap would do. No…we had to actually take a bite of the soap and chew and chew and chew. To this day I cannot stand the smell of Dial soap. Lying was not usually an option, but there were times when one of us had had enough and would either fake a confession or turn someone else in. On this particular instance my brother said that I took the pickle in the middle of the night and ate it. Thanks a lot. I of course denied it, so she punished us both. The punishment? Pickles, pickles, and more pickles. She went out and bought a case of Koshers, and my brother and I had a plate of pickles for breakfast the next morning, pickles for lunch and pickles for dinner. She thought she'd cure us of our taste for pickles I guess. And then came the dessert—Dial soap for the lie.

On another occasion she came into the kitchen just as my sister and I were finishing up the dishes. I was drying a wooden spoon on my pants leg after dropping it on the floor. There aren't many kids in this world who haven't done that, right? Well, my stepmother went ballistic! After beating me with the spoon until it broke in half, the whole time ranting and raving about germs and cleanliness, she proceeded to empty every cupboard and every drawer in the kitchen and I had to stand there and wash and dry every dish and utensil in the house.

Another thing we endured was what I call "night raids." I will try to describe one that I remember. It happened on a Saturday night. Our stepmother had lined our bedroom floors and hallway with newspapers before leaving for a "gig" (that's what she called her singing appearances at bars) telling us that she would know if we had gotten up at all. My sister Dee had to go to the bathroom so badly that night that she tried to walk along the baseboards to the baby's room, went to the bathroom in a diaper, put it in the diaper pail, and carefully made her way back to our room. Can you picture it?

~†~

Imagine…it was way past midnight. We had fallen asleep after a long evening of reading the newspapers around our beds and trying to tune out the baby's cry from the next room. I woke up in the early hours of the morning to the sound of papers being rustled and shuffled. I groggily, gingerly lifted my eyelids to see my stepmother opening and closing the dresser drawers, setting out our clothes for tomorrow's Sunday service. The closet door opens. The hangers rattle and then silence. A foreboding, heavy silence. The calm before the storm. I know what she has in her hands before a word comes out of her mouth. Last Sunday I was in a hurry and instead of hanging up my new dress the right way, I folded it over the hanger. The scream rents the night as I'm yanked out of my bed by my hair. It takes a flash of an instant for her to have the dress off the hanger and the hanger across my backside—not aiming, not caring what part of me she's hitting. The whole time the hanger is beating my body, her words are beating my mind and the little girl in me cowers under the blows. "What else do you have in that closet that you haven't taken care of?" She throws the hanger down, pushes me to the floor and begins to empty the closet of all its contents, ranting and raving the whole time. When the closet is empty she goes to the dresser, empties all five dresser drawers onto the pile and then stands with her hands on her hips, face beet red, and although she is out of breath she manages to hiss, "Clean it up!" and leaves the room.

On the way out the door she hears the boys scampering to their beds. Big mistake. She yanks them both out of their beds and sends them flying down the stairs. I hear the yelling commence again as I slowly begin to fold my clothes and put them back in my dresser. Silent tears fall on my nightgown. I know the boys are downstairs crawling back and forth across the rug in the living room. They will go back and forth across the oval brown braided rug for hours, until their knees are bruised and near bleeding. She's done it before. It's her way of keeping them off their feet, keeping them humble, keeping them afraid of her. Keeping us all afraid.

Chapter 6

In and Out of Cages

I should tell you, we were evil children! We really were... when we could get away with it! That doesn't mean we deserved what we got. No one deserves to be beaten. No behavior warrants abuse no matter how terrible. However, imagine what kind of kids you would have if for the first six or more years of their life there was no discipline at all. They were pretty much left to fend for themselves. But for momentary times of caging, for lack of a better picture, they are left to run wild and are used and abused when noticed at all. What would an animal be like if you treated it like that? This new home was just another cage. We were fed and watered and dressed up and put in a cage. Momentarily taken out to be goggled at by family, friends, and strangers and then stuffed back in the cage. If there was even thought of misbehavior, we were taken out and beaten.

There were times, however that we got out of our cages. Summer time for example. There came a point when we grew older that our stepmother would lock us out of the house for the entire day.

Let me tell you, when those times came we were terrors! We were given the chance to run free and do as we pleased and we thought we wouldn't get caught. My brothers and sisters and I did some terrorizing in the neighborhood until word started reaching back home of snakes on doorsteps and frogs thrown through windows. We were terrors! Weekends, when we weren't taken to the bar to sing and dance for the audience, and sit on the old men's laps, we were left with babysitters. I feel sorry for our babysitters. If any of you are reading this narrative and are saying to yourselves, "I remember babysitting for those monsters on Wilbur Street!" I do apologize.

I know we were awful and when my stepmother had enough of our antics while they were away, she would resort to drastic measures. She tried locking the doors of our bedrooms. That didn't work. She tried piling mattresses and box springs outside the doors so even if we got them unlocked we couldn't get out the door. It was fun climbing over them! I've already told you about the newspapers that she would line the entire floor and hallway with. I don't know why we believed that she would know if any of the pages were moved and that the babysitter would hear us walking on the paper. It was probably the fear of her that made us believe whatever she said.

There was one babysitter whom I will never forget. I don't know if she was just some kid from the neighborhood or a relative, but I'll never forget what she did the night we decided we were going to run away. My stepmother had a "gig" that night and she must've found a way to lock the doors because we couldn't get out of our rooms that night. I've already told you about "the closet" that was in our girls' room. It was a long deep closet that actually had another door that connected it to the boy's room. When we were locked in our rooms we would go back and forth between rooms through the closet. This particular night, we were locked in, but we had a plan. We had had enough of "The Witch." The boys' window went out onto the roof above the front porch and it was from there we were going to make our escape. The lot fell to me to jump first. I'm not a very brave person but I was much more of a tomboy then. It took some persuasion, but finally I jumped from the roof and landed on my tailbone! I landed so hard my head hit the ground between my legs and boy, was I in pain. So much for our escape.

The babysitter we had that night was so awesome! She heard us come in through the back door and when she heard the whole story, she brought us into the living room and took care of my pain the only way she knew how, with a bag of ice and a pizza! Then she said, "I won't tell on you, if you won't tell on me." She knew how much trouble we'd all be in if my stepmother ever found out about this. She must've known of the abuse, too, because that night she called protective services. It was a good thing she did for we were all beat pretty severely that night and I don't even know why. Maybe she found out about the runaway attempt? Who knows? She didn't always have a reason; she was just always angry. I've seen pictures of my brother that were taken at the foster home he went to soon after the runaway attempt. He was so covered with welts he looked like he had the chicken pox from head to toe. You would have to be a pretty angry person to inflict that kind of abuse and pain on another human being, especially one so small.

But it wasn't all abuse. There were the "normal" times too. It was the longest I had been in one place in my young life. Same house, same school, same parents. I wonder what my life would've become if I hadn't had someone to teach me how to take care of myself physically as an adult. I don't do all the things we were taught, or not to the extreme we had to do them. For example, I don't brush my hair a hundred strokes two times a day anymore. I don't brush my teeth with baking soda three times a day and I don't take a carbon pill every morning with hot water to prevent sickness. However, the basic principles were very helpful!

Also, holidays are huge to me, especially Christmas. One reason is because I have wonderful memories of us making gingerbread houses and going Christmas caroling with hot chocolate to follow. On our birthdays we were made king or queen for a day, were given the day off from chores, were allowed to pick what we wanted for dinner, and were served like royalty. Yes, life was good at times, and at times life was hell. What made this woman so extreme?

I've never tried to figure out what made my stepmother tick. I don't know how she grew up or what kind of pain she had to endure throughout her life. I know that she grew up in a small town in Iowa. We would go there in the summer and help her parents with the restaurant they ran. I don't remember much about those times except wrapping potatoes in aluminum foil for the restaurant and playing in her parents' back yard. They seemed like pretty nice people to me, but then again, were these just moments of "normalness" in what was an abusive situation for her as well? She was married once before she married my dad. What was that relationship like? Was he abusive? Did he have an affair with someone else? Don't you wonder about people, especially the people who hurt you? What makes them so angry and bitter that they take it out on everyone around them? I don't know, but I wish I knew more about her world. Then again, I think…what difference would it make? Would it make the memory of the abuse any less painful? If her life totally "sucked," did it give her the reason or excuse needed to abuse me and my brothers and sisters? NO!

Absolutely NOT! There is never an excuse to berate, belittle, beat, and abuse children…ever! I guess I just want to know why. I want to know that there was some other reason for the abuse and that I wasn't treated the way I was just because of who I was. We were evil children, remember? Wild Things! But really, was I that awful? Did she hate me or did she hate herself? Did she hate my life or did she hate hers? Was she trying to make me miserable because she was so miserable herself?

Maybe "why" is the wrong question. It does seem to be the first question we always ask in any bad situation though, isn't it? Why me? Why them? Why now? Why not? Why, Lord, why? Perhaps I need to start asking myself some of the other W's: Who? What? When? Where? Who is this situation affecting? Every situation affects more than just you or me. Every decision we make, every choice, every action—they all affect other people. So I need to stop looking only at my own pain and see who else is affected. What is really happening? What can I do about it? When is it going to end? When am I going to stop letting what happened in the past stop me from living in the present? When am I going to use this to learn or help others? Where am I going to go from here because I can't stay where I am and I can't go back to the past?

Where am I going to go from here? I'm going to start asking myself some of the other W's, stop having a pity party, and move on!

Chapter 7

For Those Tears I Died

There was one tragedy that happened during the years we spent with my stepmother that I am sure added to her pain and anger. It was the summer I turned ten years old. Our parents had gone out of town for the day. They were supposed to be going to an auction in a town a few hours away, and they said they would bring me back a bike for my birthday. I had never had my own bike before and was very excited about the possibility. We kids were staying at a babysitter's house for the day and that is where the tragedy occurred.

The babysitter lived just down the road and we were at her house a lot. She was a crazy, wild kind of lady who lived in a tiny garage apartment next to her parents' house. She loved to listen to records and sing and play the tambourine. Her husband was a mechanic and a hunter who owned several hunting dogs and once brought home a raccoon for us to try to raise as a pet. I'm not sure what parent in their right mind would leave their children with people like they were. They had two children of their own and I can't begin to tell you the stuff that went on in that house! Let's just say, there were very "adult" situations happening while we were there usually right in the next room without closed doors. But they were probably the only people my parents could find who were crazy enough to care for us after we scared off all the babysitters in the city!

There were seven of us kids now after my dad and stepmother had two children together. They had a son, my half-brother, who was just two-and-a-half-years-old at this point and a daughter, my half-sister, who was about to turn one. I remember on this particular day being inside the babysitter's house getting ready to feed the baby when the babysitter wanted me to run along to the store with her. We hopped in her white 4x4 and started backing out of the driveway. There was a bump like we had run into something, so the babysitter stopped the car and got out to look around. When she didn't see anything, she got back in the truck and continued backing out of the driveway. What she didn't see until she was completely out of the driveway and until it was completely too late, was that my two-year-old little brother had been playing in the dirt along the side of the driveway. That was the bump that she heard, and now his lifeless body lay half on the lawn and half on the driveway. My little sister Dee saw him before we even had a chance to get out of the truck and she ran to him and took him in her arms. To this day I still can picture her, sitting in the driveway, wrapping her arms around his tiny helpless body and rocking him in her lap. He died a few hours later. He was only two years old.

I'm not sure how I would ever handle a death of a child, but my stepmother became more angry and so much more aggressive in her treatment of us. We were put in a foster home once again while she went through parenting classes and counseling sessions and then they sent us back home to live with her and my dad. All the classes and counseling in the world would not have helped. The abuse didn't stop but seemed to escalate. The older we got the more out of her control we were. For six years, we lived like this.

No matter how often we were interrogated, accused, berated and beaten, I know now that I had an advocate in heaven who literally felt my pain. Was He stopping the abuse? No. Did He feel my pain with me? Yes, I believe He did. He knows about pain. He knows about humiliation. He knows what it's like to be bruised and bleeding. He took all the painful words and insults that were hurled at Him and instead of returning insult for insult, He hid the words in His heart so that He could know the pain I felt. He was there holding my hand and crying with me. It was for my tears He died.

> You said You'd come and share all my sorrows,
> You said You'd be there for all my tomorrows;
> I came so close to sending You away,
> But just like You promised You came there to stay;
> I just had to pray!
> And Jesus said, "Come to the water,
> Stand by My side,
> I know you are thirsty, you won't be denied;
> I felt ev'ry teardrop when in darkness you cried,
> And I strove to remind you that for those tears I died."
> Your goodness so great I can't understand,
> And, dear Lord, I know that all this was planned;
> I know You're here now, and always will be,
> Your love loosed my chains and in You I'm free;
> But Jesus, why me?
> And Jesus said, "Come to the water,
> Stand by My side,
> I know you are thirsty, you won't be denied;
> I felt ev'ry teardrop when in darkness you cried,
> And I strove to remind you that for those tears I died."

Chapter 8

I Know the Plans
I Have for You

It is surely not difficult for you to see how the people and some of the situations I was a part of were morally rotten. It is obvious that most of the circumstances I found myself in during the early years of my life were extremely objectionable. But maybe you are asking where God and the good are in all of this. Can't you see it? You have to look past the belts, bruises, and belittling. Crane your necks around the carpet burns, closet cleanings, and Comet. Can you see the little girl sitting on the rolled up rug drinking sugar water from a bottle and eating creamed corn out of a can? Where would that little girl be if she had spent these last seven years being passed from house to house, abuse to abuse, no one caring whether she was clean or dressed or fed? Where would she be?

Where is that little girl now because she spent seven years in that house? She is sitting here talking to you. Letting you know that I've been there. I know what it's like to be beat until you're bruised and bleeding. I know what it means to try to hide it and lie about it to the neighbors and the kids at school. I've been physically, sexually, and mentally abused by all the important people in my young life. I've asked the question "why me?" a million times and a million times more until the answer begins to flow over me like the waves of the ocean crashing against the rocks. The answer: Satan, the Prince of this Age, the ruler of this world, is in charge down here and he has a plan for our lives. We don't like to admit it, but it's true. The Bible tells us this and when we let that fact sink in, and when we begin to realize his goals for our lives, it fits. He doesn't want us to be happy. He doesn't want us to grow and mature and reach out in kindness to others. He doesn't want us to survive. Satan's plan for us is failure and ruin, returning wickedness for wickedness. Will he win? Will his plan succeed? It will if we don't take the time to look back and listen with our hearts. God was there. At every turn, at every bend in the road, in every situation, His hand was and still is, working in our lives; Satan is not the only one with a plan for us! "'For I know the plans I have for you,' says the LORD. 'They are plans for good and not for disaster, to give you a future and a hope'" (Jeremiah 29:11 NLT).

Max Lucado writes in his book *When God Whispers Your Name*:

> Perhaps your childhood memories bring more hurt than inspiration. The voices of your past cursed you, belittled you, and ignored you. At the time, you thought such treatment was typical. Now you see it isn't. And now you find yourself trying to explain your past. Do you rise above the past and make a difference? Or do you remain controlled by the past and make excuses?
>
> Will we choose to see the good among the evil? If we do, we will not only survive this wicked, evil plan Satan has for us, but we will thrive! We will be able to "Bloom where we are planted!"

I went online this morning just to see whether I could find the words to the song my stepmother made us sing in church. I found a website that had the words printed on a lovely ocean backdrop with little lighthouses shining their beacons in between each stanza. Then music began to play and the original artist of the song, Donna Fargo, began to sing! The chorus was very familiar but the words to the verses were long forgotten. I'm sure the irony of the words were lost on my son as he read them over my shoulder, but it stunned me as I listened with tears flowing down my cheeks.

> You can't be a beacon if your light don't shine.
> You can't be a beacon if your light don't shine.
> There's a little light in all of us by God's design,
> And you can't be a beacon if your light don't shine.
> How can you ask for truth when you do not truthful live?
> How can you ask for forgiveness when you don't forgive?
> I don't mean to bring you down or speak to you unkind.
> But you can't be a beacon if your light don't shine.
> How can you ask a child to be honest and true?
> When he can only judge what's right by what he sees in you?
> How can you offer vision yet walk around blind?
> You can't be a beacon if your light don't shine.
> May God's love surround you, may you find a brighter day.
> May He grant you the peace you seek in every way.
> God's light burns in every life, yours and mine,
> And you can be a beacon if you let it shine.
> You can be a beacon if you let it shine,
> You can be a beacon if you let it shine.
> There's a little light in all of us by God's design,
> And you can be a beacon if you let it shine.

So what happened to the wicked stepmother? Well, there was a man from our church who was a photographer. It probably began with him taking her picture for her band. She had an affair with the man, got pregnant, and had an abortion. We were there the day my dad found the abortion papers in his bedroom closet. We knew things were going to change and soon. Emboldened by the thought that this marriage and all that it entailed was near an end, we began to plan our "escape." It was like the prisoners at the concentration camps when they knew the war was almost over, and they began doing things they would never have dared do before, saving their own lives and the lives of those around them. We began making secret phone calls to our stepsister's dad for him to come and get her. We wondered what would happen to our little half-sister and whether we would end up back with our mother. But after a few days of whispered hopes and impossible plans we were abruptly pulled back to reality.

The day began with my stepmother yelling at my little sister Dee to come down the stairs and Dee said, "No." I think we were all in shock but our stepmother acted quickly and angrily, yanking Dee down from about five or six steps by her hair. My oldest brother, Rusty, finally snapped. He attacked my stepmother and with his hands around her throat I thought for sure he was going to choke her to death. He must've been about fourteen or fifteen years old. I ran out the door and down the street for help, but before I got very far down the road, she had gotten away and into her car. As I watched the car blow past, a wave of relief swept over me. I somehow knew that we'd never have to see her again, and we never have.

Chapter 9

Where the Wild Things Are

And now comes the happily ever after, right? Wrong. I was very sorry to discover and now to tell you that my life did not automatically, instantly become "It's a Wonderful Life." The truth is my dad had no clue how to take care of four kids, let alone cook and clean and run a household. My stepsister had gone to live with her real dad; my stepmother had taken our half-sister with her so that left the four of us with dad and no cage. We became, well, do you know the book about Max and the Wild Things? In the story, Max is sent to his room for being wild and that very night his room turns into a jungle complete with an ocean and a private boat for Max. He sails off "through night and day and in and out of weeks and almost over a year to where the wild things are. And when he came to the place where the wild things are they roared their terrible roars and gnashed their terrible teeth and rolled their terrible eyes and showed their terrible claws..." (*Where the Wild Things Are* by Maurice Sendak). We became like the Wild Things in Max's world and there was nobody there who even cared to tame us or take care of us. We were fending for ourselves once again and in between times trying to kill each other. We really had some of the worst fights you can imagine. There was furniture being thrown, knives being thrown, at one point there were even brothers throwing sisters across the room. The beautiful world that my stepmother tried to create was, as my sister would say, "tore up from the floor up!" We were missing school, terrorizing the neighborhood once again and probably one of the worst things, we were reunited with our mother.

We spent almost a year going between two homes with neither parent willing or able to care for us. Our dad was still living in the brick house on Wilbur St. and the place was trashed! Social Services was called on more than one occasion because of the mess and because there was no food in the house. Our mother was living across town in a broken down duplex in a scary neighborhood. We stayed with our dad during the week and went to school. Well, sometimes we went to school. On the weekends we would walk back and forth between the two.

It was so hard on me because I really wanted to belong somewhere. This going back and forth, back and forth, was driving me crazy. It was an awful time for me as well because I was quite attached to my father. It was hard for me to realize that he really did not care whether we were with him or not. I don't know what it is about dads and their daughters. I have two daughters of my own now and I still don't understand the dynamics of it all. But the truth is, I worshiped and adored my father. The rest of the kids gave me an awful time about it. I felt my mother especially disliked the "father/daughter" thing. I'm not sure why, but she showed her displeasure and encouraged the others to do so as well, as you will see.

I'm thinking of one weekend in particular. Rusty, Randy, Dee and I had left dad's house again to walk to our mom's place for the weekend. It was quite a long walk, too. I didn't realize how far it was until a few years ago when my husband, our kids, and I just happened to end up in my old neighborhood while visiting with friends. We had just passed my mother's old place when I asked my husband to drive to the old house on Wilbur Street. "It's just right around the corner," I told him, "we used to walk it all the time." Well, it wasn't just around the corner and I'm still amazed at how far we used to walk and how often!

On this particular weekend, I really didn't want to leave dad's place and make the long walk again so I dragged my feet the whole way. When we finally got to my mom's house the others told her I was sulking so she made me sleep in the car. My brothers and sisters enjoyed that immensely but my mother didn't think that was punishment enough. For the next hour or so she had them administer different forms and methods of torture and humiliation. The car I was in was an old junker. It was covered in rust, one of the tires was flat, and the front driver side window would close only part of the way. It closed just far enough so they couldn't put their arms in to unlock the doors. I had locked them when I saw that my mother was getting angry and talking to the others about what they should do to me.

Unfortunately the window opening that was too small for an arm was just the right size for a garden hose. They put the hose through the window, spraying me until I was soaking wet and shivering. Then they went in the house and got eggs to throw in on me, laughing and teasing me. At the same time, my stepfather was working on getting a door unlocked with a coat hanger. My brothers had just begun spitting in the window at me when my stepfather got the car door opened. My mother dragged me out of the car, into the house and threw me down the narrow wooden stairs that led to a cold cement basement where I slept on a damp and mildewed cot the rest of the weekend.

~†~

What makes people that cold and heartless? What brings a people to a point that they actually enjoy bringing other people pain? And the biggest question, where is God and the good in this situation? Can I tell you I don't know? Because I don't. This is still one of the most painful memories I have. Worse than the sexual abuse, worse than the beatings and night raids. Why? Because it was more betrayal than abuse. I really felt betrayed by the only people I thought I had in this world as allies. My sister and I were best friends. We fought like cats and dogs but I looked after her and stuck up for her! We were both tomboys and climbed trees, caught frogs and pulled pranks together. My brother and I were the "Wonder Twins." There was an old TV show about brother and sister twins who would put their fists together and say, "Wonder twin powers …activate!" And then they would take the forms of different animals or things and save the world! My brother and I did this so much it was a joke with my family. We looked a lot alike, too, and he was only a year older than I. We were close. All of us stuck together and were there to help each other get through the rough times in our lives, especially the past seven years. For them to treat me like this was a pain not easily forgotten.

It is tough to understand and to rid myself of the pain of that night. It is one of the things I am still working on. Why? Why not let it go, forget it, ignore it? Well, I think mostly because it still makes me angry. Barbara De Angelis said, "The more anger towards the past you carry in your heart, the less capable you are of loving in the present." I believe that is true and also, I so want to see God's goodness in every situation in my life. This makes me take the memory out of mothballs and look at it once again and say, "Where were you God?" He was there, I just know He was.

Sometimes I need to choose to look at what didn't happen. I didn't stay all night in the car. That would've been awful to be cold and wet and have my hair and face covered with raw egg all night long. I was sent flying down a whole basement flight of stairs to a cement floor below and was not hurt. That is amazing to me now. The laundry was down there so I could clean up and change clothes. Those are things I can look at as blessings in the midst of curses.

And I'm beginning to think that God needed to empty my life of the people and things that I was counting on to get me through this life. I needed to realize at some point that what is in this world is not enough to get me through it. I needed God and Him alone.

The problem was that my life and mind were so filled with people and things, no matter how corrupt and dysfunctional, I couldn't see past…well, the past. The past is what I clung to; it was the only thing I knew. I held tight to my brothers and sister, to my home on Wilbur Street and I fiercely clung to my dad. This was my world. It was broken but I didn't care. I wanted to be able to dig my roots down deep and stay forever with what I knew, no matter how messed up it was.

That was not God's plan for me. And perhaps it could only take the times in the cars and cages, being treated like an animal especially by those I was closest to, that God could draw me away from my world into His. He so longed to draw me into His arms, wipe the blood off my lip, wash the egg out of my hair and the spit out of my eyes and tell me He loved me. I'm sorry to say that I just wasn't able to see it or hear it at that point in my life. But I'm glad He didn't give up on me.

"Treasures" by Martha Snell Nicholson helped me look back at this process with better understanding:

One by one He took them from me,
All the things I valued most,
Until I stood there empty-handed;
Every glittering toy was lost.
I walked earth's highway grieving.
In my rags and poverty
Til I heard His voice inviting,
"Lift your empty hands to me."
So I turned my hands toward heaven,
And He filled them with a store
Of His own transcendent riches,
Till they could contain no more.
Then at last I comprehended
With my stupored mind and dull,
That God could not pour His riches
Into hands already full.

Chapter 10

Daddy's Little Girl

Can you guess the main thing I was hanging onto? My dad. I've said before that I'm not sure what the whole father/daughter thing is all about. I'm not sure what made me so attached to this man. He was not a big part of my childhood. I really don't remember him at all until we moved in with him and his new wife (my stepmother). But I adored him. I wanted to do everything with him. If he ran an errand, I wanted to go with him. If he was sitting out in the red station wagon listening to Howard Cosell, I wanted to sit out there with him. I'm not sure why. He wasn't really that outgoing or overly friendly. He was a quiet man and when he did talk it was usually teasing or rough. When I told him my head hurt he'd say, "If I had a face like that, my head would hurt too!" Every time he was at the door I came running up, asking him where he was going. "Crazy" was his usual answer, and he would leave without another word. I can't blame him for wanting to get out; maybe that's why I wanted to be with him so much. I envied the fact that he could just walk away and be somewhere else by himself, even if it was just out in the car listening to a ball game.

After my stepmother left and the divorce was final, my dad did begin to take us places. We went bowling and fishing but mostly we hung out at bars. We kids played the video games, shot some pool and did the clay duck hunt game while dad drank and played Black Jack. It seems messed up, but these were some of the best times of my life.

I suppose a man can live alone only so long without needing physical companionship. This is where my life did a crash and burn. This is where everything I clung to as my world crumbled before my eyes. I fell asleep on my dad's bed one night while he was up late watching TV. I woke up to him climbing out of the bed beside me. I physically pushed the hair out of my eyes and mentally pushed my thoughts and memories of what had happened between us that night deep down inside me. The only thing I let out were the tears that fell silently that day and many days after. How else is a thirteen-year-old girl supposed to deal with such things?

A few weeks later, I was with my sister at the babysitter's house. They were in the bedroom talking and I walked in to join the conversation. They were talking about my dad, joking about the babysitter having had sex with him. I stood there in utter shock that turned to a nauseating dreadful sensation as my sister shared her experience (but that is her story and not mine). Then they turned to me. I didn't say a word, but my ashen face must've given me away. The babysitter said, "I need to get you two out of there!" and she did.

Unfortunately it turned out that we were sent to my mother's, which was always a mistake. Simply said, she did not care for us. Could not? Would not? I don't know, but she did not. She didn't care if we were fed or clothed, if we were in school or running the streets at all hours of the night. I don't know whether my mother loved me. Most parents do love their children in whatever way they are able. She just didn't care. Can you love and not care? I haven't figured that one out yet, but I do know that being under her "care" was never a good idea because she just didn't care. Fortunately, we weren't there long and within weeks we were taken to the halfway house once again to wait for placement in a foster home. Before long my brother Randy and I were placed in the same foster home. We would go together to the place they set up for visitation with our dad and we'd sit there for an hour or more, time and time again, waiting for a dad who would never come. He never came to see us again.

I was looking through my old pictures the other day because I needed an old photo for a Chaplain Wives' Coffee, and I found a darling picture of me in fourth grade and also a picture from about ninth grade. I had saved this picture and was going to give it to my dad for Christmas that year, but I never saw him. The picture had this written on the back:

Dad, Hi, how are ya? Me, fine! I didn't know what to get you for Christmas sooo I hope you like this! I hope you understand why we're separated! It'll all work out for the best in the future! Really! I hope I see you more often! I miss you a lot and I miss (believe it or not) being teased! And being Daddy's little girl!

Love you. Always, your daughter, Robin D.

I bawled all the way through reading those words, even after all these years. The pain of my dad leaving me is very real. Is there anger? No. I can honestly say there is no anger or frustration attached to any of the memories of my dad. God and I have worked on this area of my life more than any other. That whole process may have to wait for another time, another book perhaps. Let me just say that the process began with trying to see God as my Heavenly Father.

Chapter 11

Like, Totally, For Sure

The foster parents I lived with in part of eighth and ninth grades had a house on the upper east side of town and they had no children of their own. My brother, Randy, was placed with me in this home but he didn't stay there long. He was a "runner" as they say in the foster care world. He didn't stay in foster homes long and was always on the run. He had a good reason for running in this instance, but that's his story and not mine. I, however, with my "bloom where you are planted" attitude, settled in to this new life and began learning what it meant to be spoiled. I had my own room for the first time in my life. A room complete with king size bed, TV and stereo/record player (yes, they still had records then). In fact one of the first things I bought with my own money was the Michael Jackson "Thriller" album! I had nice new clothes and a fancy wardrobe to keep them in. This was the early 80s and my wardrobe was complete with reversible raincoat, ducky shoes, Izod shirts, and my first pair of Lee pinstripe jeans. I was "like totally" becoming a preppy spoiled teenager, "for sure!" Thoughts of the old life were slowly being pushed aside.

The foster parents, Mr. and Mrs. G, were "church people." They went every time the doors were open: Sunday morning, Sunday night, Wednesday night, campouts on the weekends, and more. It seemed like we were doing "church things" a lot. It was during all these meetings and activities that I began to hear phrases like, "Our Father in Heaven," "O God my Father," and "Heavenly Father." This was new for me and it was something I really wanted to understand. Because my dad was so important to me and I missed him so much, I began to think about what the church was saying. Maybe God could be my new father. The problem came when I tried to match up what they were teaching about God with what I thought a father should be like. It just didn't make sense.

The church we attended taught that God was an angry God and that every time we did something wrong it was called sin. I could handle that, but not the idea that every time we sinned, God could have nothing to do with us and we were no longer "saved." I was a young girl about thirteen or fourteen, and I "sinned" a lot. Especially now that there were a lot more rules about life. No drinking, no smoking. It was not hard to stop drinking because there was no access to drink. Quitting smoking was not hard mostly because I was still around the smell of my friends smoking. It was really the smell I was addicted to because I grew up with the smell of my dad smoking. It was the swearing that was the hardest for me to control. A lot of foul things wanted to come out of my mouth and it was very difficult to stop them. I started to learn a new vocabulary. When I wanted to swear I just changed the ending a little bit. Oh, sh…oot. What the he…ck. It was really strange to hear myself talk like this but it worked. No more "cuss" words. No more sin. Right?

Unfortunately, or fortunately rather, God does not look on the outward appearance but on the heart and the thoughts of the heart. I was still a very angry young lady and though I rarely showed it, I felt it and knew that God would not be happy with the thoughts in my head. No matter how many times I tried to do good and be good and think good thoughts I always ended up with those at youth group who were praying to be "saved" once again.

This is the state of mind I was in when I was sent back to live with my mother once again. I should applaud the foster care system in their desire to reunite families but sometimes it's just plain stupid! This time was no exception. I stayed with my mother a whole six months maybe, running the streets, missing school, fighting with the neighbors and my half-sisters and then, in tenth grade I was brought to yet another foster home. My brother, Randy, had been taken there a few months before, so we were reunited once again.

Chapter 12

A Whole New World...

The foster parents' names were Mel and Phyllis Dykstra and they were "church people," too. This time, however, was completely different. They attended a different kind of church and their home was a different kind of atmosphere than I had ever been in before. These people knew God and loved God and lived it! It was very strange for me, but very wonderful to have a whole new view of the Heavenly Father thing. This new dad was what I thought a dad should be like and he matched what the new church was telling us our Heavenly "dad" was like. God doesn't like sin, duh, but He loves us so very much that He died to help us get rid of the sin. I began learning that God looks at us like His sheep and that when we go astray, or mess up, He doesn't get angry. He goes after us to bring us back! He doesn't disown us when we sin; He cries and waits with open arms for us to come running back to Him. God as my "Father" was starting to make sense to me as I began thinking about it and seeing it through new eyes.

I remember coming home from church after the first Sunday with the Dykstras. It had been communion Sunday and this would have been scary for me had it not been for my experiences at the previous church. We had communion every Sunday there so even though this ceremony was a little different, the idea was the same and I was used to the ritual. I just watched everyone else around me, did what they did, and went home happy in the fact that I hadn't messed up. Mr. Dykstra, "Dad," had commented on how glad he was that I had taken part in communion and that I was a Christian and then he gave me a big hug. He was big into hugs, which was okay, just different. Lots of things at this home were different. There were the normal activities: meals around the table, taking the bus to school, holidays. I really never knew what made life so different. I guess it's because all these things were done with love. There were no ulterior motives. There was no anger or yelling. There were only well-placed words of praise when earned, or encouragement to improve where needed. There was no cage.

For the first time in my life, I was free to be Robyn without fear of abuse or criticism. I was free to express my thoughts and opinions and I took a lot of "me" time to figure out what those thoughts and opinions were. I took a lot of walks, went fishing and biking. Just being able to be free to enjoy the beauty of this world and come and go as I pleased, within certain boundaries of course, was such a tremendous thing for me. I began journaling and writing poetry. I was growing as a person, maturing into a young lady without thought of "what if…?" and "what next…?"

For about three years I grew and matured and was thriving in this warm, loving atmosphere that Mom and Dad had provided with never a thought of cages. I was free but I still felt very alone. Cage or no cage, there was still something within me that wanted everyone around me to be happy. So I guess in a way, I was still "playing the part" and especially at church. I think back again to those comments Dad made after church. I wish he could've seen into my heart. Although my head knew what to do and how to act to make those around me pleased, my heart still had no clue and was in such pain that it was crying out to be heard and held and healed.

Chapter 13

Boys will be Boys

I hate that saying! Hate is the "h" word in our house and as much as I detest the overuse of the word, I say again, I hate the saying, "boys will be boys"! What does it even mean? That a boy can do whatever he feels like and it's just brushed aside because he's being a boy? That is so incredibly wrong. Boys do have certain normal behaviors, I suppose, like wanting to play in the dirt, blow things up, and roughhouse, anything to get rid of the "inner aggressions" especially brought on by rising testosterone levels. I get that. I know it has to be true because of all the books and talks on the subject of boys/men. I just can't seem to be able to get past all the times in my life that "boys have just been boys" and have gotten away with it. For as long as I can remember, and I'm sure there are still things I can't remember, there have been members of the male species helping themselves to my body. There were the old men that we had to dance with when we went to my stepmother's singing "gigs," always putting their hands where they didn't belong. A foster brother pulling me under his bed and saying he wanted to kiss me like they do in the movies. A cousin who pinned me behind the water heater in the basement when we were playing hide and go seek and wanted me to show him what was under my clothes. Boys just being boys? By the time I was a teenager, my body had been used so much I didn't think I was meant for anything else.

I was hoping when I went to live with the Dykstras and started attending their church that the whole boy thing would be as different as everything else was. I was wrong. One of the first weeks at the church, one of the teenagers offered to take me on a tour of the church basement without the lights on. By the second classroom he was trying to suck my face off. I started to think that I must have some invisible sign, some scarlet letter that these guys could see and think that all I wanted was to be touched. I did have a couple of boyfriends in high school that didn't want to do more than hold hands and then, I wondered what was wrong that they didn't "want" me! Isn't that messed up? As much as I hated being touched, the desire to be shown love was even greater and love to me was physical. I couldn't help it. I loved being touched because it made me feel loved and wanted. I hated being touched because it made me feel used and dirty.

I met a guy through our quiz team that I really began to think was going to change all that. We had a great friendship. We laughed and talked and shared a lot of the same hobbies and interests. He was a fun, friendly popular guy and very good-looking. He seemed like a wonderful Christian guy with a wonderful Christian family. I was just beginning to let my guard down with him and thought that maybe it's possible to have a relationship with a guy without the whole touching thing. We held hands, we kissed, we kissed a lot actually, but that's it. Until...

We had gone out on a date one Saturday night. We were going to go to the movies, I think. We got to the parking lot of the theatre but he parked away from the rest of the cars and before the engine was even off, my heart was racing. I can't even tell you what happened next, what was said or done, but I found myself being pushed over the front seat into the back and he had somehow managed to remove the bottom half of my clothing. I never had fought back before, but I remember hitting him and telling him no and to stop. I never fought back again. It didn't do anything but make him more determined to conquer me. And when his bragging of his conquest got back to me through a friend I was devastated. Devastated and loved. You probably won't be able to understand that.

There is no way to comprehend how a person can feel both used and loved at the same time. I hated my abuser but I loved being "loved." I needed to feel loved and I hated myself for that during those many months we were together. I wanted it to stop so badly and yet I was afraid of being alone once he left me, as he surely would if I began telling him no. I tried to make him hate me. I did things poorly to frustrate him. I cut my hair short, which made him very mad. I started talking about other guys. He would come pick me up at lunchtime "to park" a couple times a week and I began telling him I couldn't anymore because I kept being late for my next class, which was true, but it was an out! I was trying so hard to end things but didn't know how. Finally things were ended for me. His parents were gone one weekend and he brought me to his house with only one thing on his mind. My mind, however, was set against it and I'm not sure what led to such determination on my part but I won. I left his house leaving my ripped pantyhose behind, in his parents' bedroom garbage can. When his mother found them on their return home, she made sure we never saw each other again.

When I was out from under the oppression of that relationship I began looking around and discovered that I had surrounded myself with boys. I had adopted all of my girlfriends' fathers and called them "Dad" and gave them hugs. I hung out with all the boys in the youth group, giving them nicknames and flirting. I even turned one of my friends little brother into my "little boyfriend." Was I that afraid of being alone? Was I that insecure with myself? Was I that dependent on the physical attention of men to feel loved? How incredibly messed up, but that's how my life was until the day I found someone to touch me in a way that would change my heart and life forever.

Chapter 14

All the Places to Love

Can I take you on a little tour of the "mansion" on Nine Mile Road where I lived with my newest foster parents, Mom and Dad Dykstra? Okay, so it's not really a mansion, but it was certainly the biggest, loveliest place I had ever lived.

Anyone driving past the brick home would note the wrought iron fence, the columns on either side of the wrap-around driveway, and the stately, elegant way that the many-windowed home sat among the immaculate lawn and shrubbery. The formal garden and green house, the fountain that flowed into a pool, the big red barn with cows grazing nearby, and the bird feeders filled with birds twittering in the shade of the ancient sycamore tree all added to the mystique of the place. It was a jewel of a house and this is where my brother Randy and I spent three years of our lives.

If you were to come in the back entryway you would see a box of freshly picked apples given to Dad by one of his customers at the feed mill that he owned and ran. There is a furnace register contraption, one of the tall old fashioned kind, piled with hats and gloves on the top and lined with boots and shoes underneath, warming themselves against the cold Michigan winter weather. You would also see that there are three more doors that lead in and out of this little entryway. The one to the right goes out to the three-stall garage. There is a set of stairs inside the garage that goes to an apartment above. The door straight ahead goes out to the round picnic table with the fountain pool to the left and the wild flower garden to the right. Grab an apple and come on through the last door, which is the back door into the kitchen. It's a clean, freshly remodeled country kitchen with a few cow figurines tucked here and there. Cross stitched pictures of a boy and girl hang on the wall next to a wooden boy swinging on a wooden tire swing and a little wooden girl with red curls rocking in a miniature rocking chair. The round wooden table with its many chairs is inviting you to sit and have a cup of tea but we must press on.

The dining room is next and although the solid, beautiful wooden table and buffet are original to the house, the lovely rose wallpaper is new and loves the sunshine that streams in from the tall windows that cover two of the walls of this room. We go through the arched doorway into the formal living room next. The massive front door is on your right and the open wooden staircase on your left. Just past the front door is the wood-burning fireplace with a picture of a woman harvesting grain hung above the mantle. There are two couches in this room, a rocking chair that was Grandpa's, and two matching chairs on either side of the fireplace. In one of these chairs is where Dad usually sat at the end of his long day at the feed mill. He would put his feet up on the footstool, read the paper or write in his "thankful" journal and wait for Mom to call that dinner was ready. The final room on this floor is what Mom calls the "sunroom" because all three walls are nothing but windows! The room is complete with TV, stereo, two Lazy Boys, and the baby grand piano. It is also where the Christmas tree would be displayed every Christmas.

Head up the stairs with me, but notice as we go that every inch of the stairwell wall on the left is covered with pictures. These are the pictures of every person who has been a part of the Dykstra family. From the Dykstras' own children: Mike, Laurie and David, to those who may have only spent a month or a few weeks as "part of the family." They are all represented on this wall and it seems like their eyes follow us up the stairs, the great cloud of witnesses, so to speak, all with their own story to tell. All of them have one moment that they share in common and they would all whisper to you, "I was loved by this family."

The first door you come to at the top of the stairs is my room, but let's go past there for now to take a peek at the rest of the house while we're on our little tour. Just past my room is the bathroom with green tiles from floor to ceiling and my rubber ducky under the bathroom sink! Then Mom and Dad's room with bed, TV, and a wall of built-in bookshelves filled with books. Around the corner is a little den where we sit and play board games like Stratego or Scrabble. At the end of this room are glass doors that go out to a little sunroof. There is another bedroom whose occupant has changed three times since I've been here and then the stairs that go up to the third floor. My brother, Randy, has a bedroom up here and his own bathroom. There is also a spare room that has a bed, lamp, and all the Nancy Drew and Hardy Boys books you could ever want, along with a few other books. This spare room is just one of the many places to love in and around this house.

I have a favorite children's book written by Patricia MacLachlan called *All the Places to Love*. It talks about different family members and their favorite place to be in their world. The Grandpa loved the barn best and the good sweet earth. The Grandma loved the woods and streams and the mom in the story loved to climb the hill to where the blueberries grew, where it felt like you could touch the sky. It's a lovely story and it reminds me of all the places I loved at the "mansion" on Nine Mile Road.

On a beautiful fall day, you might find me in the front yard sitting under the sycamore tree journaling. (Under, not IN, climbing was strictly forbidden!) In the spring, I might've been walking the barn road to go visit with the new litter of kittens in the barn or to toss a bale of hay down to the cows from the loft. You may have looked for me in the Formal Garden. There was a white wooden swing between two giant pine trees where I loved to sit and swing and read *Anne of Green Gables*. There was also the fountain pool that was big enough to swim in when the weather was hot. I just loved to sit in the little side pool at night and listen to the water's soothing melody as I watched the stars and made a wish on each as they started to shine, one by one.

Inside the house I had some favorite spots, as well, like sitting in front of the fireplace sipping hot cocoa, especially in the cold February weather. The piano is another place I might have been sitting and trying to pluck out "Fur Elise" again instead of practicing "Spanish Guitars" from *John Thompson's Book One* like I was supposed to. I loved playing Scrabble in the den with Randy or lying on the bed in the third floor spare room reading a Hardy Boys mystery.

There were many places to love and at any given moment you may have found me in one of these places writing, laughing, reading, playing games, or just being pensive. But like any typical teenager, I also spent a lot of time in my bedroom at the top of the stairs. It was a beautiful room. Mom and I redid it in pale pastel colors, yellow and pink, and there was Precious Moments wallpaper on the walls. It was lovely. If I could, I would throw myself across the pale yellow polka dotted comforter and listen for the sound of the fountain outside my bedroom window or the Baltimore Oriole's bright song that was always such a wonderful source of joy and peace.

I would lie there and remember one night in particular that I spent in this room. It was a cold night in February and it is the night that I remember finally crying out to God. I remember it like it was yesterday and fresh tears fall as I bring the scene to mind.

Chapter 15

He Touched Me

Stop outside the door and listen. There's a young teenage girl, not quite seventeen, on the other side crying her heart out tonight. There is nothing lovely about her thoughts. No beautiful pictures in her head of places to love. She's sad—the deepest of sad. As Anne of Green Gables would say, she's in "the depths of despair" and I'm not even sure I can tell you why. I'm not sure how life amid such loveliness and light could get so dark and depressing, but it has. She is lying across her bed weeping bitter tears over pain and heartaches and loss, and she is feeling utterly alone.

She has removed a razorblade from a shaver in the bathroom and she is slowly, methodically passing the razorblade over her wrist again and again. Gently. Timidly. She is not serious about ending her life quickly but each time she presses a little bit harder. The physical pain this causes is not major or new. She has etched a few initials of past boyfriends in her arm before and physical pain is nothing compared to emotional pain. Each time the blade passes across the smaller of the two veins, scenes pass across her mind and she uses those images to convince herself that there is not a single person in the whole world who would care if she dies. Some of the scenes are trivial: one of her girlfriends spending all of her time with her new boyfriend, another girlfriend's rude comments about her new hairdo, and scenes from the fight with her latest boyfriend. When her mind is done with trivialities, it moves to the deeper issues.

The truth of the matter is she is scared, afraid of being alone and without family for the rest of her life. She has not seen her birth father in years! Her birth mother has just sent a letter to the court clearly stating her wishes not ever to be contacted about her children for any reason. Her brother, Randy, has moved out and moved on with his life. Her sister Dee is 15 and pregnant and living from place to place. She doesn't know where Rusty ended up. The sadness comes from the fact that she never sees any of her "real" family anymore. Everything about her life in the past has changed and although it has changed for the better, her mind is clinging tightly to all that it remembers and holds dear. She doesn't want to let go of the past and she has convinced herself that she is the only one who cares about her birth family anymore. Never mind that what she once called "family" was messed up and mixed up and just plain wrong. The point is: what is life without family?

Mom and Dad Dykstra have been awesome and she loves them dearly but even then she has convinced herself that they didn't really love her, not as "their own." (Your mind can convince your heart of anything when it is already so sad.) Besides, she wasn't part of their "real" family and High School graduation was just a few months away, and then what? Then she too would be going off on her own, to what? With whom? She was going to be all alone and it seemed to her that there was no one who would even care. She would kill herself, saving herself the pain of change. Would it matter? Would anyone care? Would they miss her? No, she is convinced. Her life would end and it would not matter to a single soul.

As the blade passes over the artery one more time a small trickle of blood begins to flow with the tears and it is at this moment that she hears God crying too. He is saying, "It matters to me! I will miss you, Robyn. I care about you and I know you're hurting. I am here with you. I am your helper, your healer, your heavenly Father. Won't you come to me now?" He stands with outstretched arms and the girl runs! In body, she is on her knees wrapping her nightshirt around her wrist to stop the bleeding. In her heart, she is running to wrap her arms around Jesus to stop the pain.

If there was ever a time in my life that was a "happily ever after moment," I think this night would have to be it.

> He touched me, O he touched me,
> And O the joy that floods my soul!
> Something happened, and now I know,
> He touched me and made me whole.
> Shackled by a heavy burden,
> 'Neath a load of guilt and shame,
> Then the hand of Jesus touched me,
> And now I am no longer the same.
> He touched me; O he touched me,
> And O the joy that floods my soul!
> Something happened, and now I know,
> He touched me and made me whole.

I was safe and secure in the arms of my Heavenly Father at last. And although there would still be pain, there would now be peace. Nothing could change the past or suddenly erase the scars that it causes, but memories and scars both fade with God's healing touch.

> initials of past boyfriends
> across my arm were scrawled
> a scar across my wrist was left
> when life wasn't worth it all
> those scars have disappeared
> and others of their kind
> but deeper scars remain

they are the ones in my mind
the tears have fallen
the memory fades but
the pain still lingers on
lord you said you gave your love
to take away my sin
please come and take the pain away
and remove the scars within
it's you who has brought me where I am
only you can set me free
5-8-1988

Chapter 16

Ruminating and Revenge

I needed to realize, as I did soon after this poem was written, that the pain I was experiencing was not all from scars but from open wounds as well. There were many parts of my heart and mind that were still suffering from the open, festering wounds caused by anger, bitterness and resentment. There are so many words that describe the outcome of the different circumstances we find ourselves in or the feelings we develop toward the people that have been a part of those difficult circumstances. Anger, bitterness, resentment. We use these words interchangeably without really thinking about what they mean. This is how I've come to view these terms and how they work themselves out in my life.

God has planted a seed in my heart and He wants it to grow and produce fruit so I might "taste and see that the Lord is good." The problem comes when I allow the weed of resentment to grow up around me and within me. Resentment is what happens when we allow ourselves the luxury of ruminating. You know what ruminating is don't you? It's what cows, camels, and the like do. They swallow something only to keep bringing it back up to chew on for awhile and then swallow it again. We take a painful situation in our life and swallow it only to bring it back up again and again. It is the act of reliving the memory to its very minutest detail every moment, allowing the vine of resentment to grow up and around the true vine of who we are in Christ. We keep this ritual up until the vine bears the fruit of bitterness. Instead of tasting of the fruit of the Spirit, we take a bite of bitterness and allow ourselves those feelings of hurt and helplessness. Why? I have no idea. It makes completely no sense to me whatsoever but it is what I do.

Max Lucado describes bitterness this way in *He Still Moves Stones*:

> Bitterness is its own prison. The sides are slippery with resentment. A floor of muddy anger stills the feet. The stench of betrayal fills the air and stings the eyes. A cloud of self pity blocks the view of the tiny exit above. Step in and look at the prisoners. Victims are chained to the walls. Victims of betrayal. Victims of abuse. The dungeon, deep and dark is beckoning you to enter… You can you know. You've experienced enough hurt… You can choose like many to chain yourself to your hurts… or you can choose, like some, to put away your hurts before they become hates. How does God deal with your bitter heart? He reminds you that what you have is more important than what you do not have.

When I first read that I thought, "Yeah, right!" He makes it sound like it's as easy as putting away your toys. But then I thought, "In a way, that's right." I was hanging on to my past even still. Those festering wounds—I was the one keeping them open and painfully fresh. I kept taking out those memories like they were my favorite playthings. It's warped isn't it? But I don't think I am alone in this ritual. Even when I began to go through the process of giving pieces and parts of my past and painful memories to God, I would still keep one tiny piece for myself. I would from time to time take out that tiny bit of bitterness as a memento of my old life. The taste of bitterness is surprisingly addictive. I don't know why else I would want to relive the pain of the past. The other problem is that bitterness has the same power that any drug does to make us lash out in anger.

I see anger as the action word in this whole scenario. Anger reminds me of a tree in the Harry Potter books. The tree is an ancient Whomping Willow that lashes out and pummels anything that comes near it. Anger is like that. We revive and relive painful situations until they become so strong and prominent in our lives that they begin to bear fruit. We taste that fruit all the time and become intoxicated by the bittersweet sensation of being wronged. But at the same time we feel we're entitled to our pain and possibly our revenge. If anyone approaches us or questions us while we are in this state, we become like the Whomping Willow, lashing out irrationally at all who come near.

Speaking of revenge reminds me of a character, Inigo Montoya, in the book-made-movie, *The Princess Bride*. There was a man in this character's young life who killed Inigo's father and then wounded Inigo, leaving him with two long scars on either side of his face. Inigo Montoya spent the rest of his life studying and planning and preparing to meet his archenemy to say to him at long last, "Hello. My name is Inigo Montoya. You killed my father. Prepare to die." When he finally found his enemy and was ready to face him, this is all he could say over and over and over. Revenge had consumed his whole heart and mind. After his enemy was dead, there was nothing left for him. His whole life was spent for that one moment. What a waste! And I began to see that happening in my own life.

I had a recurring thought and dream that plagued me for years. I wanted to shoot my stepmother. I imagined it so many times and so many different ways. What the situation would be like, what I would say, what I would do, and the different kinds of guns I could use. I didn't realize how much those thoughts were consuming my heart and mind. Dad had guns locked up in the basement that he would use to go skeet shooting or to get rid of the pesky red squirrels that were always trying to find their way into the attic.

One day I was stopped mid thought—I was thinking about what I would do if I took one of those guns. The Holy Spirit was helping me see where my thoughts were, and it scared me. I became afraid of the anger that was building up inside of me against this woman. I didn't want my heart and mind to be consumed, like Inigo Montoya's, by bitterness or anger or the thought of revenge.

That fear has affected the rest of my life. It has affected how I have raised my children. Besides the fact that I won't have guns in my house at all, my kids were never allowed to play with guns or watch shows with guns. It has been only a very few years since they've been allowed to play with water guns! They have also been taught to fix things right away. If you have something against your brother or sister, tell them, fix it, and give them a chance to say they're sorry. I have over and over again tried to teach them not to hang onto past hurts and not to try to seek revenge. Hopefully my experiences will help them make better choices and keep their hearts and minds clear of the clutter of past hurts.

Looking backward takes up a lot of energy and I did eventually get tired of looking back, focusing on the past, and ruminating on old hurts. Eventually I was ready to "taste and see that the LORD is good" (Ps. 34:8). And once I did, I was ready to have God help me with my addiction to bitterness. How did He do it? As Max Lucado said, God reminded me again and again that what I had was far more important than what I didn't have anymore. Every time I was tempted to take a little bit of bitterness to chew on for awhile, I had to purposefully choose to put it away, put it behind me. Instead of constantly looking back and remembering the pain of what I had gone through and the family I had lost, I began opening my eyes to what God had given me in the here and now.

Robyn's second-grade school photo

Robyn had written a note to her dad
on the back of this tenth-grade photo.

Family photo with stepmother and baby brother in 1979,
a few months before he passed away.
Robyn is at far left, second row, beside her stepmother.

Billy and Robyn's engagement picture by the
sycamore tree in front of the "mansion" on 9 mile.

Family photo with Mom and Dad Dykstra,
taken in 2005 before Billy's second deployment.

Chapter 17

My Angel Mother

I have said a lot about my new dad and how that relationship has helped me see how my Heavenly Father cares for me. What about my mom? Although she showed me God's love as well, the greatest thing she did for me was to show me what the world thinks of me and to help me change my view of the world.

I somehow think that the majority of our self-esteem comes from our mothers. Think about all the "greats"—men and women who have done awesome things in this world. We've heard time and time again from their biographies and from their own mouths what awesome mothers (or some other very influential woman) they had in their lives. There was the motherly voice saying "great job," "you can do it," "I believe in you." George Washington said, "My mother was the most beautiful woman I ever saw. All I am I owe to my mother. I attribute all my success in life to the moral, intellectual and physical education I received from her." Abraham Lincoln is quoted saying, "All that I am or hope to be, I owe to my angel mother." I have a dear friend who used to tell her children every night, "God has a plan for you." How awesome is that? To know every day of your life that you are not worthless, your life isn't meaningless, you're not a random piece of creation, God created you with a specific purpose and you're going to go out into the world and do amazing things!

That is one of the greatest things a mother can do for her child. A father points the child up to God. A mother points them out to the world around them. There are always exceptions, and more often than not, this building up and sending out does not happen as it should.

The same friend said to me one day, "You know what, Robyn? You're really a miracle. We're both miracles because of what God has done with our past and what He's doing in our lives right now." I've thought about that and I've decided that my "miracle" is that I was given a dad who pointed me up and I was placed into the care and keeping of a mom who built me up to send me out into the world.

I think you've gotten a pretty good picture of the moms I've had up until Mom Dykstra. What did I learn about myself and the world from them? That I was worthless. Ignored, caged, beaten and abused, I had nothing that the world wanted except perhaps my body which they took and used without my being able to stop them.

It was this girl who stepped gingerly, timidly into the warm inviting kitchen at "Nine Mile" and heard one of the sweetest sounds in the world—laughter. Not a loud, mocking, ridiculing laugh but a comforting, gentle laugh that made me feel like everything was going to be okay.

When I messed up, which I did quite often (I had a lot to learn about life and relationships), Mom would smile, shake her head and say, "Robyn, Robyn. Do we need sermon fourteen again?" And she would laugh. Not at me but with me. I didn't have to be afraid of being belittled for my mistakes or beaten and caged so I would never make the mistake again. Mom helped me see that people make mistakes and that we need to learn from the mistake, try to see things from the other person's perspective, and laugh at ourselves while we're at it.

One of my biggest problems was that I was so used to fending for myself and fending off the world that I had become quite a selfish, self-centered person. It was not only that I thought I had nothing to give the world, I didn't think I owed the world anything. It had been nothing but harsh and cruel and I wasn't able or willing to see that there were others hurting and in need. Mom helped me to open my eyes to the people around me and allowed me to see that who I was as a person could affect those around me for good or for evil. Who I was becoming as a person was important to God. He wanted to use me in the world to care for His people. God had a purpose for me.

Not only that, but I was loved for who I was. It was unconditional, no strings attached. Mom is not a huggy-kissy kind of person. Not like Dad is. It's taken me years to put my finger on it, but the other day I just sat and bawled as I let the fact sink in that my mom loves me. Simply loves me. Not for what I bring to her but, I think, for who I am as a person and for what I can bring to the world to show them God's love.

Max Lucado was right; it just took me awhile to be able to look beyond what I had lost to see what I had been given.

Thank You Lord for Dad
Accepting the loss of my father
Wasn't something I wanted to do
Even though you gave me a new dad
I wouldn't accept this gift from you.
There were just too many hard times
There was just too much pain
I couldn't forget the memories
I saw the loss and not the gain.
Who was this new dad anyway
Why was he loving me so
Why was he always giving me hugs?
Questions whose answers I didn't know.
But Lord you kept on working
Making clear your plan for me

Helping me to deal with the past
And to accept it gratefully.
Thank you Lord for my dad
And the loving care he gives
Help him know that I love him too
Being called his daughter is a privilege.
    6-2-1988

Thank You Lord for Mom
I know I've been ungrateful in the past
For the moms you've given me
And I know I've had no right
But to accept it quietly.
But even when I don't praise you
And fail to see your plan
You gently lead and remind me
"Child, you're in my hand."
I truly thank you, Lord
For all that I have today
But especially for my mom
Who loves me in a special way.
Even though she didn't carry me
Those first nine months of life
I know she carries me deep in her heart
Through good and through strife.
All those times she never knew
How important she was to me
How much of a Mother she was
And how much of a "mom" she'll always be.
    5-8-1988

Chapter 18

Off to College

Well, I couldn't stay in my lovely safe shelter forever. Eventually I had to go out into the world on my own. The first step was going off to college. The college I chose, with the help of Mom and Dad and the church youth pastor, was Word of Life Bible Institute. WOLBI was a very strict but very camp like one-year Bible college.

It is set in upstate New York and is nestled among the Adirondack Mountains with some of the lower peaks reflected in the small lake that is a part of the campus, Schroon Lake. It was a calm peaceful atmosphere untouched by the world. The dorms were chateau type buildings among the trees, all forming a circle around the main campus. Council Hall was the main building where we met for all our classes and any other special meetings. It was a large wooden building with wooden stadium benches for seats. The desks were removable wooden desktops that fit over the backs of the benches. All meals were served in the dining hall with assigned seats and attendance taken at dinner. It was a strict school with harsh rules not only about PC (physical contact) and dating but also with regard to personal devotions and physical and spiritual well being. Some of the rules were: no PC at all, no dating without a third party, a letter or phone call home each week, physical activity journal turned in weekly, and your room inspected on a daily basis. Also, personal devotions were to be done and recorded in a daily journal to be placed on the corner of your desk.

When we broke any of the rules, demerits were handed out. When the demerits added up, there was extra duty. I had my share of demerits. I even have some given to me by my husband! (We met at WOLBI, but that's a different chapter.) My kids get a kick out of that and the fact that I had to peel potatoes for two hours!

What a wonderful year this was for me. Not only was I being immersed in Scripture and the history of Christianity, but I was also meeting new people and reaching out to the world around me. All students were required to have a weekend ministry. There were inner city programs and music and drama clubs. I was placed in a local church ministry at a church called Perth, which I absolutely loved. Every weekend our group would board the bus or van and head to the church. On Saturday we would go around visiting kids and their families and inviting them to church. On Sunday we would ride the bus and pick up those who had said they would come. We visited pretty much the same families every week so we really got to know those kids and their families and the situations they had to live in. There were some that lived in situations that were so similar to my own experiences growing up that I just wanted to wrap my arms around their precious little lives and never let them be hurt again. It was such a life-changing time for me to be able to see that there were other children in the world who were hurting and that I could love them, if only for a minute.

We were able to be a part of these kids' Sunday school classes as well as other ministries. It was here that I fell in love with the church. When I saw all that Christ was able to do with this one body of believers, it motivated me to go back home and be involved all I could in my home church.

There were two major difficulties during this time for me. The first was when my grandmother passed away. This was Dad Dykstra's mom. She didn't live near where we did and I didn't know her very well but I knew she cared for me and prayed for me every day. She was the first person close to me to die since my baby brother had died so many years before. I spent a lot of time crying over this loss and the fact that I couldn't go home to be with my family.

WOLBI campus, as you can probably imagine with the lake and trees, was very beautiful and had many places where one could walk and sit and think. I had a favorite spot down by the lake where I loved to spend time thinking and writing, reading and praying. I sat on the big rock facing the lake with the cold wind blowing through me as I wrote:

It's so cold here. I stand alone in the darkness of my mind. The wind blows so hard and brisk. It seems to go right through me. I wonder if this is what death feels like. So cold and dark and lonely. Where can I go from your presence, O Lord? Depths of the sea you are there—in the darkness of the lightest day—you are there. I try not to be sad—I try to hide the tears. I know you see deep within me—I could never comprehend how well you know my heart and my mind. Lord, walk so close to me today. I need to feel your strong arm—I need your strength today. And everyday.

P.S. Tell Grandma I love her.

Chapter 19

In His Arms of Love

Perhaps it was the pain that my grandmother's loss brought to my heart and mind that also began to stir up other memories. Memories that were too far buried to be fully remembered. I don't know if this was the cause, but there was something that brought about the other difficulty during my year at Word of Life and that was the flashbacks.

I had no idea I was having flashbacks then. I still don't fully understand flashbacks now, but something would trigger a memory or make me feel like that scared, caged little girl once again and I would curl up into a little ball and cry like a baby. I wouldn't always cry. Sometimes I would just stare wide-eyed and rock back and forth until someone would come and pull me out of wherever I had gone in my mind. I looked up "flashback" just now and the dictionary says that a flashback is "a recurring, intensely vivid mental image of a past traumatic experience." Maybe there is some other terminology I don't know about, because I don't think I was seeing any vivid mental pictures. I was just shutting down so I wouldn't have to. Whatever it was called or whatever the cause, it was only a small beginning to the episodes I would have later in my life. I'm thankful that they began there in that loving Christian environment which brought compassion and not ridicule.

~†~

At the end of our year at WOLBI we had a soul winning class that basically taught us how to use the Bible to talk to people about God and His love. We were taught the "Roman Road." In the back of this book, I've written it all out for you. At the end of this particular class period we were asked to break up into groups and practice. The three girls in front of me turned around and began to practice on me! Remember that I had come to God in the privacy and convenience of my own bedroom. I never had anyone point a finger at me and say, "You need Jesus." I had never heard the verses spoken directly to me about how God loved me so much that He sent His one and only Son to die for me. It was incredibly powerful stuff and it scared me to death! I began to wonder if all this time I had just been playing the part. There was something in the verses about knowing in your mind the right answers but also needing to believe in your heart and then confess with your mouth. Did I have only the head knowledge and not the heart knowledge? Whatever it was that struck my heart that day and made me run out of the building in tears, also made me stop in my tracks just outside the door and cry out to God once more.

Although this was the first time I had heard these particular verses spoken right to me, it wasn't the first time that God had taken the scared crying little girl that was locked up inside me and wrapped me in His arms of love. And it wouldn't be the last.

Lord I'm really glad you're here.
I hope you feel the same when you see all my fear,
And how I fail, I fall sometimes.
It's hard to walk in shifting sand.
I miss the rock, and find I've nowhere left to stand;

And start to cry.
Lord, please help me
Raise my hand so you can pick me up.
Hold me close, Hold me tighter.
I have found a place where I can hide.
It's safe inside your arms of love.
Like a child who's held throughout a storm,
You keep me warm in your arms of love.
Storms will come and storms will go.
I wonder just how many storms it takes
Until I finally know you're here always.
Even when my skies are far from gray,
I can stay; Teach me to stay there,
In the place I've found where I can hide.
It's safe inside your arms of love.
Like a child who's held throughout a storm,
You keep me warm in your arms of love.
"Arms of Love" by Amy Grant

This was the first song I taught myself to play on the piano. I would practice it over and over during my hours off that summer at WOLBI until I knew it by heart and would sing it at the top of my lungs when nobody was listening, of course! I just loved the thought—and still do—that when the storms of life are raging around me I can crawl up into my Daddy's lap and hide in His arms of love.

Chapter 20

Looking for Love in All the Wrong Places

My year at World of Life was a wonderful time of getting to know myself and getting to know my Savior. But the truth, is I left Word of Life Bible Institute with a broken heart.

I left confused, and it has taken me a while to figure out what God was doing in my life in the matrimony department. I mentioned that I met my husband, Billy, at WOLBI. It isn't called Word of Life Bridal Institute for nothing! They have even changed the words to the theme song just for fun from, "How did you feel when you came out of the institute walking with the Lord?" to "How did you feel when you came out of the institute walking down the aisle?" Contrary to popular belief, however, most ladies don't go off to Bible college to find a good Christian husband. It wasn't one of my goals either. The fact was, I was just getting over a broken relationship.

I'm not sure who started the tradition of getting pre-engaged, or why, but the Christmas before I graduated from high school, the guy I was dating told me his intentions to marry me. He asked if I would wait for him through college and he gave me a pearl "promise" ring. I could not have been happier—for a moment.

I don't know what made me open my eyes to what this relationship was really like or to see this man that I had made a promise to as he really was. It must've been a God thing. He was a wonderful Christian man; his family was a very loving dedicated family who lived in the town where Mom grew up. In fact, every time I saw my grandpa during that time he would ask me, "How's Byron Center?" It was so cute. My whole family liked the guy. He was just very "clingy." He loved being near me every minute of every day. What girl wouldn't be flattered? He spoiled me rotten but never took the time to get to know me.

He assumed he knew what I would like and bought it for me, did it for me, brought me there, etc. I couldn't tell him how I felt, for I hardly knew myself. It was just nice to feel loved and not used. I am thankful that when I finally looked past the lovely thought that somebody would want to marry me even though I was "used goods," I had a clear picture of what my life would have been like. Besides having to spend every Friday night with his entire family playing cards and eating pizza, I would've become a wife and lost who I was as a person. It was scary and I ran. Not far, but far enough to give him back his ring and tell him we needed time apart. At college we had space between us, and we needed space, so I was able to see even more clearly. I knew he was not the man I needed to marry. And certainly, finding a replacement was the furthest thing from my mind.

~†~

When I met Billy, I knew he would be a great friend, a true kindred spirit. With thick, bushy red hair and a smile that lit up his bright blues eyes, this West Virginian's love for the Lord and for people was contagious! It was wonderful getting to know him and hearing about all the amazing things he wanted to do with his life. One of the first times we sat down to have a real chat, it was about all the things that we had in common in our lives and in our common desire to reach out to kids. We were on the same local church ministry team for awhile so we spent a lot of weekends together, ministering and getting to know each other. We wrote notes, sent cards, walked and talked. God used all the little day-to-days to knit our hearts together. I was still writing poetry and he did a bit too. We had a mutual friend who played the piano and sang. We had "our" song that she wrote and sang for us. She also put some of my poems to music to sing for Billy. We were connected but not mushy in love. Part of the problem was that Billy wasn't looking for love and he was not ready for the commitment of marriage.

The other problem was that God wasn't through teaching me about love. I still thought love was a physical thing. Think of how all the men in my past showed love. As messed up as that was, it taught me love was physical. Well, there was no PC (physical contact) at WOLBI—I mean none! I got demerits once for tapping the bus driver on the shoulder to ask him a question. Well, if I couldn't hold Billy's hand, then I could at least wear his hat or his coat. Anything to feel physically close. It didn't matter, though, because I soon realized that the more I tried to get close to Billy, the farther he went away from me. And so friends remained friends and although our hearts were permanently knitted together, it would take awhile for God to bring us physically together. He had major changes to make in both our lives.

WOLBI is a yearlong program that includes doing a summer ministry either at the college or somewhere else. Billy's ministry was going to take him back to his home state to be a youth pastor. My summer ministry was to be done there at the college counseling high school age girls and housekeeping. Billy and I parted ways with a hug and he boarded the bus with his hat and coat and left me quite crestfallen at having to say goodbye to a very dear friend without any hope of ever seeing him again.

Bear with me as one more guy enters the picture. The pearl ring guy from B.C. was not my first love. Billy was not my first love. Before them and through all those little high school "romances" there was Rob.

A year ahead of me in school, a constant in the youth group, and my best friend's brother, Rob was my first and secret love. He was my ideal. Handsome in his own right, his looks were improved by his gentlemanly behavior and gracious manner to all living things. He was quiet but could be the group clown, quick to laugh and to bring a smile to others with his quick wit.

Rob and I never dated before I went away to Word of Life although we did a lot together in the youth group and we made great Rook partners. (Rook is a card game that is played with teams and Rob and I were unbeatable!) It wasn't until my year at WOLBI that Rob started making phone calls from Moody Bible Institute where he was attending. Through those phone calls and a few letters, our relationship was growing and strengthening so that at the same time I was sad for saying good-bye to Billy, I was also looking forward to seeing Rob back at home.

Rob and I spent a lovely week together after we both got back from college on summer break. We had lots of walks and talks, quiet times listening to the birds at the park or laughter at get-togethers. By the last day of our time together I was convinced that Rob wanted to spend the rest of his life with me. We met that last day before I had to go back for my summer ministry at WOLBI, very early in the morning to go fishing on Hubbard's Lake. After a lovely quiet morning on the lake, Rob turned to me before we left and said, "You won't go and marry anybody else while we're away at college will you?" And I said, "You never know, I might!" with a little impish grin. That was all the understanding we had as we parted ways.

I have no idea what happened those following few months to change Rob's mind, but by the end of the summer he had gone back to Moody early instead of waiting to meet me like we had planned. There was no note and no phone call. A week or so after I got home to find him gone already, I got a letter in the mail saying that our relationship was over and that he knew he could never marry me. I don't know if I could describe to you the devastation this brought to my heart. What happened? What was God doing? It took me months of crying, writing, questioning why, God? Why?

It took me awhile to see what God wanted to teach me through this painful situation.

Rob's dad pulled me aside after choir one night to talk. I was very close to Rob's parents, with his whole family, actually. His sister was one of my best friends and I spent a lot of time at their house. His little brother was my "little boyfriend," and I still have the stuffed ball he made for me in school. When Mr. R. pulled me aside that day, I was not expecting to hear what I did. He was basically having a pity party for me. He said, "It must be so awful being a foster kid. You must be so lonely with nobody to love you." These words were so powerfully painful. The knife of truth cuts the deepest especially when thrust in by someone we trust and respect. The truth in his statement wasn't that I was unloved and alone. I wasn't. I knew that. I was confident in my Heavenly Father's love and my mom and dad's love for me. The truth was that I was acting like I was unloved. I was still playing the part of the poor foster kid instead of taking on the role of a Child of the King. In my relationship with Rob, as well as all the others, I was still looking for love. I was longing for the security of never having to be alone. I was "looking for love in all the wrong places" and in all the wrong ways and for all the wrong reasons. I didn't need someone to feel sorry for me. I didn't need someone to cling to me or be physically close for me to feel loved. I didn't need to settle for the first person who made me feel wanted nor did I need to cling to what I thought I wanted.

I needed to wait on God. Rest in my Father's love for me and cling to Him and Him alone.

Chapter 21

First Comes Love...

When I was confident in my Father's love and had stopped "looking for love in all the wrong places," that's when God brought Billy back into my life. Eight months after we said good-bye at WOLBI, I got a letter from him. Letters turned to phone calls—long, long distance phone calls. Calls led to visits, and a friendship grew into romantic love over the course of a year. In December 1989 we were engaged to be married. I am still amazed at how God took all of those "love" experiences in my life and used them to mold me and teach me the full extent of what it means to love and be loved.

May 11 was one of the most beautiful days of my life. The day before was the wedding rehearsal and the rehearsal dinner which all went wonderfully. That night, Billy and I stood outside the back door to the house—out by the wild flower garden—holding hands and staring at the stars. Billy broke the silence by saying, "There's one thing we haven't practiced yet—the part that comes after 'you may kiss the bride.'"

There have been 5 great kisses since 1642 when Saul and Delilah Korn's inadvertent discovery swept across western civilization. The precise ratings of kisses is a terrible difficult thing often leading to controversy because although everyone agrees with the formula of affection times purity times intensity times duration, no one has ever been completely satisfied with how much weight each element should receive. But on any system there are 5 that everyone agrees deserve full marks. This one left them all behind." From *Princess Bride* by William Goldman.

Here is proof positive that God had changed my heart and my mind on the love subject. Billy and I did not kiss until the night before our wedding. We didn't even hold hands but once or twice until after we were engaged. You may think this was no great feat, considering we were separated by hundreds of miles most of our courtship, but you couldn't be more wrong. We had plenty of time alone together on dates and on the road trips we took back and forth from Michigan to West Virginia. I was in relationships before where we couldn't make it from point A to point B without "making out" at each stoplight! Billy and I spent lots of time expressing in words the anticipation we had of expressing our love physically and were both very thankful for the strength God gave us to wait.

Chapter 22

Then Comes Marriage

The day of our wedding dawned glorious and except for a small thunderstorm that halted the filling of the fountain pool, everything about the whole day was perfect: the ceremony, the flowers, the music, the reception. I floated though it all until I found myself sitting next to my husband on the small love seat in our hotel honeymoon suite looking through wedding cards and talking about the day. It's a good thing that the wedding was videotaped because you miss so much when your mind is in the fog of the day. My kids and I sat and watched the video the other day and it was so fun to look back! The biggest thing I noticed was how young everybody looked! Then it was seeing the faces of loved ones who have since passed away. The thing that struck me the most while watching this time were the words my dad said to me at the end of the aisle when asked, "Who gives this woman to this man?" This is what my dad said:

> Robyn, this is the day that the Lord has made. We will rejoice and be glad in it. I just want you to know that your mom and I

are so thankful that we had the opportunity to have these past six years to be a part of your life. We count it a joy and a privilege that you've been able to live in our home. We love you so much.

Billy, we give Robyn to you to love and cherish as God's special gift. As we've seen her grow and mature, we are so thankful that she also grew in the Lord and that she met someone who also loves the Lord. As you begin your life together, we are just trusting that you'll live a life of service for Him. We want you to know that you will always be in our minds and hearts and above all in our prayers. Take good care of her for us will ya? She's a special gal and we love you both.

Man! Is God good or what? He took this scared little girl, placed her in the care and keeping of a wonderful Christian mom and dad and let me bloom. The little girl, who before would've only seen hatred and divorce, saw love and commitment in them, and I longed to have the same thing in my life. After much trial and error in the dating department, God sent me Billy. There we stood in the presence of God and family and friends, and as the songs were sung and the words were spoken, I knew that this was what God intended love and marriage to be. I knew He was the glue that would keep our love alive and our commitment strong. I knew God had somehow taken all the awful, hateful images and notions I had about love and marriage and replaced them with this lovely perfect picture of His love for me, and I am still amazed.

~†~

The first few days of our honeymoon were spent in Michigan and then we loaded up a small U-haul for the trip back to our new home in West Virginia. The problem came when we tried to hook the U-haul up to the car that Billy had borrowed from his pastor for the trip. There was no way to make it work and so I had to decide in a moment what I wanted with me and what I could do without until family friends could bring my things down to West Virginia a few weeks later. I was momentarily devastated. My mom made the comment to me last Christmas, "I've never seen anyone with so many favorite things!" That's me, and all my favorite things were packed in boxes in that U-haul. I didn't want to leave any of them behind.

All the wonderful memories I had were tied somehow to the pictures and stuffed animals and all the rest of the things in that trailer. My first boom box, my smiley face bank, the doll Mom made for me and the kitty pillow, all my journals and writings, at least a dozen stuffed animals, each with a special memory attached, and pictures upon pictures of all of my fondest memories. What could possibly be good about having to leave all my favorite things in a U-haul and drive away?

Physical. All physical. God was trying once again to get me to see with spirit eyes and realize that I held people and memories in my heart, not in my hand. Again and again in my life I have to go back to the poem, reminding me once again that God cannot pour riches into hands already full. I needed empty hands held out ready to receive the people that God was about to fill my life with. Painful but necessary.

When my precious things finally arrived, about a month later, one of the first things I did was to take out my bag of stuffed animals and give them away to the group of girls who had come into my home and into my heart.

Sometimes God has to empty our hands of stuff or they will be too full not only to receive but to be used by Him to reach out to others with His love. So, I've learned to put it down, put it away, or give it away (which drives my husband and my mom absolutely crazy!) so that my heart remains full of lovely memories but my hands are empty and ready to do His will and receive the far greater riches of His blessings.

Chapter 23

Then Comes all the Tough Stuff

Married life is tough. I don't know what I thought it was going to be like; if I had thought about it all. I'm not a future thinker by any stretch of the imagination. Even if I was, I don't think I could've imagined that within the first few months of wedded bliss my husband would leave his full-time job as youth pastor and try to provide for us by working part-time bagging groceries. My perfect world would not have included financial struggles, emotional baggage, spiritual battles, or the amount of tears that were shed as we packed up, left our little garage apartment, and moved across town, the whole time trying to celebrate the joyous news that we were expecting our first baby.

All the real struggles with my past, the panic attacks, and the flashbacks did not hit me full force until after I had my first daughter. I'm not sure why that is. One counselor explained that all the fears I had as a child I began transferring to Katie and eventually to all my kiddos. All the panic and fear I felt growing up in the insecure circumstances I found myself in, were all coming back to me, gripping me in the heart, paralyzing me where I stood. Common, ordinary circumstances became terrifying. Trust was banished and fear reigned supreme. I was terrified of my past.

~†~

Imagine if you will—it's about two o'clock in the morning and a young lady is trying to start her car to go pick up her husband from his second shift job across town. The car starts fine but every time she puts it in drive, the car stalls and rolls backward a little bit and a little bit more. She begins to panic. Her hands sweat. Her breathing increases. Her chest tightens as she looks in the back seat at her sleeping six-month-old daughter. She realizes that the back wheels will soon be over the hill. In fact, as she steps out of the car, she knows that she is too late, the car's back wheels are already spinning in air and she cannot get to the back seat to get her baby out. She is in a full panic now. Standing in the middle of the road, she is crying and yelling for her husband. "Billy! Billy! Where are you? Help me, Billy!" She knows he's clear across town at work but she screams his name anyway one last time and then she begins thinking of the neighbors.

Not calmly, rationally, but in a full rage of panic, OH GOD, OH GOD, OH GOD, Who can help me? There are only a few houses up here on the side of the hill, but there was an elderly widowed man who lived across the street and doted on baby Katie. She needed his help now and she ran to his door. When he didn't come to the front door or the back door she began pounding on windows and yelling, "HELP me! Please help me! My baby. My baby's going to die!" Finally the man came out in his pajamas and slippers, carrying a baseball bat. It's a wonder he didn't call the police, but he hadn't and he did his best to calm the young lady down. He climbed into the driver's seat of the car and on the first try, was able to get the blue Oldsmobile's four wheels back on solid ground. After thanking him and apologizing profoundly, she got back in the car and cried and shook until the panicky feeling went away and she could drive to go pick up her husband.

I was only a little late picking Billy up from work that night but I was still a mess emotionally by the time I got there. That was only one of the many episodes I had during those stressful two years in West Virginia. Why not let him drive himself to work, you may ask? It was actually worse when I didn't have the car. The car meant I had a little control over when Billy was coming home. Those nights I was left home alone with no car, I would not sleep. I wouldn't let my daughter sleep. I would keep her up all night. I would keep the TV on all night and I would pace. When Billy was late getting home from work, I would panic. I would stand in the middle of the road in my pajamas and slippers and cry and yell. Where are you? Why aren't you home? Oh, GOD! Is he dead? Is he not coming home?

Craziness, huh? Just the other day I told my husband that I felt like that young girl standing in the middle of the road in her slippers in a full panic, not wondering where he was but wondering where God was and where the good in my life was.

I don't know why it is so easy for me slip away from what I know to be true. I knew my husband wasn't dead somewhere but what I know doesn't always change how I feel. I've been struggling for years trying to figure out what makes me panic so. What makes me throw everything I know to be true out the window in favor of what I am feeling at the moment? I should have known my husband wasn't going to leave me on the top of that hill with our little girl all alone, but I didn't. I still don't.

One of the first songs I taught my kids as we sat and watched at the window or front door was…

Where is Daddy? Where is Daddy?
Where are you? Where are you?
Hurry home quickly, very, very quickly.
We miss you. We miss you.

I should have known. I should've known he wouldn't leave. I should've been able to trust the man I chose to marry. Where was the trust?

When I left Michigan I thought I had left behind everything I knew. Suddenly my world was turned upside down and I had no solid ground to stand on. Husbands leave. Dads abuse. God is a distant father. And I was in a deep pit of despair.

When I was standing in the middle of the road yelling "Billy, where are you!" I was really yelling, "God, where are you?" I had left Him in Michigan. I knew Him best at Nine Mile in all the places to love and in the peaceful places at WOLBI. That's where I could feel His arms around me. That's where I could crawl up into His lap, but not here. Not now. God was far away and I was lost and alone in West Virginia. I wanted my husband but I wanted him to be what God had been to me all those years since I cried out to Him in my sunshiny bedroom on Nine Mile. Billy was not my Heavenly Father and as much as I thought I needed him to be that, I needed to realize, and still from time to time need to be reminded, that he is my husband and not my God. As much as I long to have that vision fulfilled in my life of my husband loving me like Christ loved the church, I need to know and make real in my life constantly that small word "like." Like Christ loves, not instead of Christ's love or in place of God's love. God is my Heavenly Father everywhere I live, not just in our special places to meet. Jesus loves me no matter where I am or what is going on in my life. As much as I desire my marriage to look like that, I should never desire it to replace that.

All those years of fear. All those hours spent worrying and wondering if I would be alone or unloved, hurt or abused.

It started with that young lady on the hillside in her slippers crying out to God not to leave her alone and it ends with her realizing that He has never left her side.

Chapter 24

Cleaning House

I know I said that when I accepted Christ into my life as my Lord and Savior, as my Abba Father, that it was a happily ever after moment. But the truth is, that it was just the beginning. The beginning of a whole new story. A whole new process. There is a great big word theologians like to use for this process, sanctification. It means to set apart for sacred use, to make holy, to purify. It's kind of complicated but not really. I like to think of it as cleaning house with the Lord along as Mr. Clean.

Saturday Cleaning

After I became a Christian I knew there were things that needed to change. I needed to clean up my act so to speak. The smoking, the drinking, the language—I've already talked about those things. I call that Saturday cleaning. People do their major cleaning on different days of the week. Or maybe they clean every day. We Saturday clean at our house. The kids and I mostly dread it, but we work together and half way through we're into the swing of things and we are all so glad when we sit exhausted in a freshly dusted, vacuumed, "Lysol-ed" house and talk about how we're going to trash it again by having company over and throwing some kind of party or get together.

I grew up with a record called "Free to Be You and Me" and on it Carol Channing does a little snippet that I paraphrase like this:

> The next time you happen to be just sitting there quietly watching TV and a lady comes on with a lighthearted smile and a friendly wink, trying hard to make you think that her soap or detergent or powder or paste or wax or bleach is the best soap or detergent or powder or paste or wax or bleach, remember nobody smiles while doing housework. She's smiling only because she's an actress and she's getting paid to make those speeches about those soaps or detergents or powders or pastes or waxes or bleaches. Your mommy hates housework, your daddy hates housework, and when you grow up you will hate housework too. Little boys, little girls, if you want all of your days to be sunny as summer weather, remember whenever there's housework to do that you do it together...

And so we put in the "Free to Be You and Me" CD and work together to clean up the stuff we can see. Saturday cleaning in our lives is like that. It's the straightening up of the little things that accumulate over the course of the week. God and I did a lot of Saturday cleaning the first year of my new life. Just dusting off the surface of things so that my outward actions to people showed Christ's light. Some bathroom talk and thoughts needed to be "Lysol-ed" away. Some spills needed to be wiped up with Bounty as I learned to apologize and put things right as soon as possible. Some stains needed the spot-bot after I did things I shouldn't have or hurt people in a deeper way. Lots of Saturday cleaning going on but no deep stuff. No dirty closets or under beds. Not yet. That would come with Spring Cleaning.

I knew what a good Christian looked like and I wanted to look the part, straighten up a little, dust a little, Lysol the bathroom, that kind of thing. One of the first verses I remember memorizing was for a musical that our youth group did. The verse said something like this: Take no thought of his appearance or the height of his stature. Man looks on the outward appearance but the Lord looks on the heart. Yikes! That means that it really didn't matter to God if the place "looked" clean. He knew what I had in the cupboards and closets of my heart and mind. So began the process of God and me going from room to room, sanctifying it, cleaning it up, making it Holy so He could use each area of my life for His glory. Painful and painstakingly slow. People don't become perfect Christians overnight, you know. In God's eyes we're perfect, forgiven, but as someone once said, "God loved you just as you are but loves you too much to let you stay that way." And so room by room, closet by dirty disgusting closet, we went and are still going actually because God's not through with me yet. He is constantly and lovingly making perfect the work He began in me all those years ago.

At first the process was not really all that painful. It was like the "27 Thing Fling" that The FlyLady suggests doing once a month. (The FlyLady is an online self-help woman who offers tips for housekeeping, such as throwing out 27 things in a tour through your house.) Not hard to go through a messy house and throw out 27 things. But as the main part of the house gets clean, it's harder and harder to find 27 things to fling. You have to look under things, dig deeper into closets. It gets tougher.

While I was still at home surrounded by loving family and fabulous friends, it was not so tough. Yes, I had tough spots to work on. I had to get out the oxy-clean and the magic eraser a few times. There were tears shed, but as time went on I realized there were some things in my heart and mind that were going to take heavy-duty detergent. There were some closets that were, and still are, so full of yuck that they're oozing black gook out from under the door. There are even some places that I don't even know exist yet. How can that be? "Whiter than snow, yes, whiter than snow." That's one of my favorite hymns. But it's a process. God knows who we are, who He's created us to be. Sanctification is the clean up process. It is getting us from where we are to who we are in Christ. A process.

Lord Jesus, I long to be perfectly whole;
I want Thee forever to live in my soul.
Break down every idol, cast out every foe;
Now wash me, and I shall be whiter than snow.
Whiter than snow, yes, whiter than snow.
Now wash me, and I shall be whiter than snow.

Spring-Cleaning

I love Spring Cleaning. Really, actually love it. I love when it gets warm enough to open all the windows and let the breeze blow through the house. I love cleaning windows so the sun can shine in once again and I love getting rid of stuff! My husband cringes when I tell him I'm going to have a garage sale because most of what I'm selling (or practically giving away, he says) is stuff that he spent his hard-earned money on because one or more of us needed or just had to have it. Hastily gotten, easily discarded. That's what garage sale stuff is and that's what Spring Cleaning is good for: letting the Holy Spirit blow through our lives like a mighty rushing wind and cleaning the windows of our heart so the light of Christ can shine in and out freely. It's a great opportunity to get rid of all the junk in our hearts and minds. All that stuff that is hastily gotten and easily discarded. What things do you see mostly at garage sales? Movies, books, clothes, and toys. I get tired of watching the same sob story over and over, so I get rid of it. No happy ending? Get rid of it. If it's too big, too small, outgrown, worn out and stained, get rid of it. All the old playthings? We've outgrown them physically and mentally. We're ready to move on past childish things. Get rid of it. When I was a child I spoke as a child; now that I've grown up, I've put away childish things. I've cleaned out the cupboards and closets. I've done the spring cleaning. I'm ready for the Holy Spirit to blow a fresh wind through the halls and for the light of Christ to shine through the windows.

Deep Cleaning

There are some things we don't touch even during Spring Cleaning. There are boxes of all shapes and sizes tucked here and there that we know we don't want to deal with just now. Maybe they've sat dust-covered so long that we don't have any idea at all what's inside them anymore. That's the tough stuff. That's worse than the bottom of the oven or under the refrigerator. No amount of Pine Sol will work on this stuff. You can't just stick it in a bowl of Oxy-clean and have it come out white as snow. You can't Shout it out or Magic Eraser it away. It's going to take something called elbow grease. Good old fashioned mental, emotional, physical, spiritual elbow grease.

Most of the time these boxes are handled by choice. We get sick of the clutter and the stench and we say, "Okay, God, today you and I are going to tackle this one!" It's tough and I should say, "Today we're going to START on this one" because most of the time the junk in these boxes and closets takes time—lots of time to clean up. I have lots of such boxes and closets in my "home." They hold the situations and memories that I've tried to take out one by one and say, "Okay, where were you here, Lord?" "What were you doing there, Father?" "Where is the good in this situation?" I don't want to be afraid of closet doors or men with beards or the sound of a belt being taken off in the dark.

I don't want to spend the rest of my life wondering about what would have been, eating through the pain that is now and worrying about the possibilities of hurt in the future. The best way that I've found for me to do that is to let God show me Himself as we clean through the yuck. Then I can see where He was in my life, how He is with me now and get a glimpse of what He can do with who I am in the future. One crammed oozing closet, one greasy slimy box at a time.

Is it easy? You know the answer to that. It is never easy. It is excruciatingly painful and as much as God wants you to get through it, Satan wants you to stay where you are. He likes the slime and the stench and he wins when you stay bogged down in the gunk and so he tries his best to block your efforts. It's his goal to discourage you in your task and trash your thoughts. It goes something like this:

The door. Remember the door of the kindergarten teacher? I so wanted to know what was behind it so I no longer had to be afraid. God and I, I thought, could go there together and just get a small glimpse through the keyhole perhaps. Baby steps are good, I thought. The problem was, Satan decided to tag along and he turned my little field trip into a fight for my life. A fight within myself. Instead of heading toward the door in my mind, I suddenly didn't want to see. I didn't want to know what went on behind that bedroom door. I have to though, I thought. I have to fight all these demons chasing me. Suddenly they were ganging up on me. Surrounding me with taunting and oppressive guilt. Circling and jeering, ever moving me closer and closer to the door. They taunt me with their ghoulish singsong voices until I'm pressed against the door banging and begging to get in. But the door won't open. Don't worry about it, just walk away. The voices change their tune. You don't have to see inside this room. You don't want to know. You don't need to deal with it, just walk away. Run away. Run. Run and hide. Run back to your cage and hide.

But I stay. I'm tired of cages. I'm still banging on the door with my fists with my head against the door, only it's the door of the shower and the hot water is pouring over me trying to wash the filth away. And then the interloper comes. I push him away all the time knowing how much I need him. I need him to hold me. The interloper is my husband, Billy. I recognize his voice. I know he loves me. He never comes to hurt me. He is with me now, trying to stop the pain. Trying to tell me that it's okay, but he doesn't understand. He doesn't know that I need him to hold me, to touch me, to show me that it's safe. I need to know that he loves me and doesn't think I'm dirty. I can only cry out in my mind, "Oh, please don't be repulsed by me, Billy. Please don't walk away. I need not to be numb. I need not to be afraid." When I come back to the "real world," I'm sobbing and exhausted and laying my head on my husband's shoulder.

As I look back on that scene, I smile a little at the thought of my husband in his army uniform soaking wet because he climbed in the shower to stop my banging head and my pain. I also have to shake my head at myself. Did I really think God was going to tiptoe with me like a little child and let me peek through a keyhole? He went through excruciating torture and then the cross to deal with the yuck of this world. Why did I expect that dealing with my past would be child's play?

Is it always this hard? No! Sometimes the memories come gently, like a soft quiet rain. I call it "raining-on-the-inside, leaking-on-the-outside," as the tears quietly escape my eyes.

Sometimes just a smell or a sound will trigger the memory. I was hit in the face a lot as a child and still to this day, that is one of the most painful things for me. I can't stand being hit in the face, even if it's an accident, like with a pillow in a pillow fight. Billy tossed me a pillow once and it hit my face. I can't even pretend to say it hurt, physically that is. It just hurt on the inside and I buried my face in my hands and cried. Again, the raining-on-the-inside, leaking-on-the-outside kind of cry and I like to think that maybe it washed away one more memory of a time when it was physically painful and meant to be.

"Feel the Nails," a song by Ray Boltz, speaks about this same concept only in terms of Christ and what He went through—His betrayal, the mocking crowds, the suffering of the Cross. The song asks us to wonder if Christ still feels the pain of those events. Does He have to relive the memories of those heart- and body-wrenching moments every time we sin? I used to get so very angry every time I heard the song! Jesus doesn't have to die over and over again! What kind of theology is that? "Once for all," the Bible says. Then one day I asked myself why? Why does it upset me so to think that every time I sin, Christ has to feel the pain of the crucifixion all over again? Well, who would want to think that? Then I realized that I am the same way. I still feel the pain. Not the exact physical pain but the emotional memories of the pain, the scars.

He must, too.

Chapter 25

We Can't Always Choose

The best way to clean out everything, every closet, every corner, is to move. My husband is in the Army, which gives us lots of opportunities to sort through and pack up. We've just recently moved to Korea and that was one of the most stressful situations in our married life. Box after box. Cupboard after cupboard. Closet after closet. We sorted and sorted and sorted. There were three different shipments. The first one went on a plane so that it would arrive in Korea about the same time we did. The second one went on a boat and it took just over a month to get there. The third went on a truck and was sent to storage. There was a ton that we couldn't take with us. No furniture, for instance. It was so difficult to go through my house and think what I can and can't live without for two years.

Maybe it would be good if we could do that with our memories and our experiences. "That's a good one, I need that right away." "That's no good, it can go in the garage pile." Like the show Clean Sweep, it would be good to go through our hearts and minds and say "keep or toss." The thing is that we have a choice. We didn't have a choice whether we went to Korea, but we certainly had a choice about what we took, what we tossed, and what we stored away. It really helped me to see what was important in our lives.

The most difficult house cleaning comes when you don't have a choice. A sound. A smell. A date. A color. In the flash of a moment you are thrust into a memory—a flashback. Sometimes that memory is still so very painful or so deeply buried that all you can do is—well, nothing. How many times in my early marriage, especially after I had children, would I find myself curled up in a ball, rocking silently or whimpering like a baby? Remember the counselor who suggested that when I had children, it awakened my childhood memories and feelings? That was especially true as my kids came to the ages I was when I was neglected or abused. The point is, I could not control it. I had no choice in the matter. I wasn't going to God with a box in hand saying, "Let's deal with this one today, God." Nope. I was just slammed with it, much like those new automobile commercials. Have you seen them? Two people are riding along in a car having a conversation and the whole time you're wondering what the commercial's about when out of no where—BAM! The car is hit by another car or truck! I jump every time I see those commercials even though I know the crash is coming. I think that's what flashbacks are like.

I wouldn't be able to tell you really what a flashback looks like except that my husband has recounted to me enough of what I say and do. When we were early married, maybe three years, we had our two girls already, 11 months apart! We were living in an apartment, a very small apartment where our couch doubled as a bed in the back bedroom so Billy could also have a place to study for seminary. It was night and I was already just about asleep when Billy came to bed. It was the unbuckling of the belt in the dark that did it and I was already shutting down when he came toward me as a dark menacing shadow. I curled up as a ball and started to rock and cry. Cry like a little baby, my husband says, and nothing he could say could bring me out of it. He couldn't hold me either because the closer he came the worse it got.

After awhile I was able to recognize somewhat what was happening. I could calm down enough to let him in and let him hold me through it. I began to trust his voice even though it was his actions that brought me panic. I was also able to know what had caused the panic. The belt, the beard, the closet door.

The point is, it's so much harder when you don't choose. So I've made myself look inside the closets and boxes, under the beds and in the attic. I've taken each memory out one by one, taken them to my Heavenly Father, and asked the questions so that I can learn to see Him—good among the grime, sweet among the stink, pure among the putrid, and never failing to be faithful.

Chapter 26

I Have Been There

Sometimes when I've attempted to deal with the pain I've had in my life I've found that there isn't always a particular person I can point a finger at. There is no abuser, no one to accuse or hold responsible. For example: the loss of a child, the death of a parent or grandparent, a house fire, things that we would call "acts of God." Different from abuse in many ways, these situations bring with them their own kind of pain.

There are some things that a heart cannot forget. It's been more than thirteen years, and I can still remember every detail about the day I received the news that my baby had died. I remember what the ultrasound room looked like and what I wore that day. The smells and sights and sounds. The image of the little peanut on the ultrasound screen. They are all imprinted in my mind like a bleak winter scene etched into a cold black piece of glass. There are some things that a heart cannot forget.

It was a cold day in October, and I was scheduled to have a routine ultrasound at my local hospital. I was about sixteen weeks along in my third pregnancy, and the doctor had yet to hear a heartbeat. It was nothing to worry about I was assured; this sometimes happens especially after multiple births, plus I had put on quite a bit of weight that might be hindering things.

I walked into the clinic, finishing the gallon of water they make you drink before an ultrasound, and I sat and waited my turn. Two minutes into the ultrasound, I knew something was wrong. The technician became really quiet and soon left the room without an explanation. A different technician came in a moment later, all smiles and friendly, and began the ultrasound again. She had a calm reassuring voice when I asked her if something was wrong, and she asked me to go to the bathroom and drink a few more glasses of water. They were just making sure that they were getting a clear picture of the baby she said.

I got up from the table and did as she asked—but was she nuts? More water? After two babies, my bladder wasn't that strong to begin with and yikes, it hurts when they're pressing on your tummy like that!

When I came out of the bathroom, there was an official looking, doctor-type person at the ultrasound machine. "Okay, Mrs. Graham, let's see what we've got going on here," he said, as he began the process yet one more time. This man had the bedside manner of a steamroller. Right away he said, "Okay, we've got a problem," and he turned the screen so that I could finally see what they had been seeing. My baby was just a tiny peanut of a thing on the screen. I was used to having ultrasounds later in pregnancy when there are clearly defined fingers and toes. There was none of that, and the worst part, the doctor so bluntly pointed out, was that there was no heartbeat. He showed me the small black spot on the screen that was my baby's heart and that's the spot I stared at numbly as the doctor explained that my baby had died. They didn't know the cause or why my body had not done its job getting rid of the fetus. Yes, he actually said those words. He told me that my OB doctor would probably give my body a few weeks to expel the dead fetus, and if that did not happen naturally, then they would have to do a D&C.

I dressed in a continued state of numbness that slowly turned to anger. He was talking about my baby like it was garbage that my body needed to get rid of! It was so unreal to me. No one could talk about a baby like that, could they? When I left the room someone handed me a paper and told me I would be getting a call in a few days with my next appointment, and that was it. I walked like a zombie out to my van where I sat for who knows how long. I don't know if I even cried. I just remember sitting there for the longest time before I remembered my two girls at the baby sitter's. I needed to get home to them and hold them tight and wait for my husband to come home from work, so he could hold me tight and let me know that everything was going to be all right.

The next few weeks flew by in a blur of tears and confusion. I didn't talk about what was happening to me because it still didn't seem real. I told my parents and one or two of our closest friends, but that's all. I struggled within myself and by myself. My baby was dead inside my "safe place," and I wanted to know why and I wanted someone, not to feel sorry for me, but to at least be able to sympathize. To be able to say, "I've been there."

The day of the D&C was awful. My husband was there with me, but when he found out that a D&C is really just like having an abortion, he was pretty upset. The pain of the procedure was intense. They did give me something that put me out for a while. When I woke up, the first thing I remember is a nurse in my face saying, "Robyn, wake up honey, it's all over. Everything is all done." And I cried. I lay there and cried and cried until I could cry no more.

A few days later I was back at the doctors for the follow-up visit. It went pretty well until I was left alone in the room with my chart. I was flipping through looking for a report to see if it said what the sex of my baby was. We never knew if it was a boy or a girl, and I wanted to know. I found the report and it was then that I realized my husband was right. The report was just listing all the parts that were found of my baby after the procedure. I really didn't understand what I was reading until it said male fetus approximately twelve weeks gestation. I ran to the bathroom and threw up.

When I got home that day I began journaling and wrote a poem expressing my feelings. I thought that writing in this way would be a good beginning of the healing process for me, but I still had to deal with people's comments. People have been the biggest roadblock to healing in my life in many different areas and this was no exception. The rude and unnecessary comments, the well-meaning comments that are hurtful nonetheless, and the questions all added together to prolong the pain of the wound. "God knows best." "You should be thankful for the two healthy beautiful children you already have." "You're not going to have any more kids, are you?" And when you think it can't get worse than that, a friend comes along that you haven't seen in a month and asks, "When's the baby due?"

There was one person during this time who did something I will never forget. My sister-in- law came over during my healing time. I was still in bed with my feet up, and she came into my room and didn't say a word. She gave me a hug and let me put my head on her shoulder and cry. There were no words of comfort, no spiritual anecdotes, nothing. She just let me cry—because she had been there.

I wish I would have known then what it took me years to learn and then to finally be able to do. God had been there as well, waiting silently, no words of wisdom, no answers or explanations, but He was there. He just wanted me to crawl up into His lap, lay my head on His shoulder and cry. And cry and cry and cry until wailing turned to sobbing, and my heart could quiet down enough to hear Him say what Mark Schultz has so eloquently put to music.

I have been there.
I know what pain is all about.
Yes, I have been there
and I'm standing with you now.
I have been there.
I came to build a bridge
so that this road could lead you home.
Yes, I have been there.

March of the following year found me pregnant once again and scared. Would I lose this baby too? Nine months later, a ten-pound baby boy joined the Graham family and brought happiness and healing to my hurting heart. Did this new baby take the place of our dear Matthew Eli? Certainly not! In fact, when I was given my "Mother's Necklace" a few years ago, the one with the little boy and girl charms, the kids all voted that I get a little boy charm with Matthew's birthstone on it. They have not forgotten him either. We have chosen to keep the place where he lives in our memories clear of the weeds of bitterness and resentment. As a result, that place has grown and matured into a lovely garden where we can go to reflect and yes, shed a few tears, but leave with peace instead of pain in our hearts.

It is what I know that God wants from me. Not just in this instance, but in all of my moments and memories. He so longs to take my hurts and turn them into something greater. I won't say rejoicing. I don't think I can ever rejoice in the loss of my son or in the many situations I was in as a child. But I can choose to see God and the good in each situation. More importantly, I can use my empty but open arms, my sympathetic touch, my healing heart, to reach out to those of you who are hurting as well, and if nothing else, I am able to say, "I have been there."

Author's note: The story of the loss of our child is written in its entirety in *Stolen Angels: 25 Stories of Hope after Pregnancy or Infant Loss,* ed. Sharee Moore, published by Dynasty Publishers, 2006.

Epilogue

Happily Ever After

I'm sitting in my Army issue standard living room chair that is covered with the same green, brown, tan leafy fabric as my couch and dining room chairs. My feet are propped up on the Army issue oval walnut coffee table, and my pen and paper are in hand preparing to write this final chapter. The page stared blankly back at me for quite awhile actually, blank but for the title written across the top of the page: "Happily Ever After."

My husband Billy leans over to kiss me good-bye before he leaves for work and notices the title. "Is that what we're living?" he says somewhat sarcastically. "Sorry about your prince charming. Most days I feel more like an Orc (those hideously ugly creatures in *Lord of the Rings*), sweaty and stinky with green blood." Yeah, Army Green, I thought to myself and then wondered along with him, "Is this it?"

I've been waiting for my life to be perfect for such a long time. I keep thinking—someday. Someday my house will be just how I like it: clean, beautifully decorated, no dirty laundry. Someday my body will be just how I want it: skinny, long hair, no bad back and no wrinkles or sagging skin. Someday my world will be just how it should be.

Someday the washer won't sound like it's going to explode, the freezer door will stay shut, the dog will scoop his own poop, the kids will do their own laundry, my husband won't smell like an Orc when he comes in from PT, the Army will send us to the first place on our "wish list," and gas won't cost $4 a gallon.

In my perfect world the cat will lie down peacefully with the dog, the kids' rooms will always be clean, and the kids will never grumble about their chores. A perfect world for me would have no deployments, no war, and no overseas assignments. No good-byes, no arguing, and no laundry.

My life doesn't look like that now. My laundry is NEVER all done! "Like shoveling in a snowstorm," someone once told me. Most of the time the kids' rooms are 'hit' as in tornado, cyclone, earthquake-hit! We've been in the Army only five years, and we've already moved three times. The first move the kids and I made by ourselves because 17 days after going on active duty, my husband, as a newly appointed Grace Brethren chaplain, found himself in Iraq. And we were left in our small Indiana town with our heads spinning and our hearts aching. Three months later I sold the house and moved three kids to Ft. Campbell, Ky., put them in public school for the first time in their lives (they were in 4th, 6th, and 7th grades), and joined a community of wives who waited and wondered as I did.

Billy was home a little over a year before he was sent back to Iraq for round two. This second deployment was harder on us because, unlike the first time, we didn't have the newness of Army life and the move and new things to keep us busy. The biggest difference, however, was that we now knew how long, how very long, a year is. Before Billy was home from the second deployment, we received the news that we were heading to Seoul, South Korea, and we'd have only three months after he returned home to prepare.

That move happened in a whirlwind of tears and frustrations and madness! We arrived in Korea, spent nearly two months in a hotel (albeit a grand and glorious hotel), were given living quarters the same week we found out we'd be moving again in four months. This time we'd be heading south to a different Army base in a town called Daegu. Yikes!

So, since April 2003, we've missed two years of celebrating special events and holidays together like Thanksgiving and Christmas, birthdays, anniversaries, first piano recitals, first homecoming dances, and first broken bone. We've moved from Indiana to Kentucky to Seoul to Daegu, South Korea. Billy's mom passed away and other relatives and friends were sick and near death. We've had to say good-bye to countless neighbors and friends as they moved away and to our own family and friends, knowing we would not be able to see them for a very long time. We couldn't even bring out dog with us. You in the military know of these pains. They are not extraordinary, but par for the course. I know this and have been handling the military life fine—until Korea. This has been one of the most difficult times in our lives. I dug through old emails to find and share part of a "Graham Family Update" that I had sent out in March after having arrived in January.

> I will thank you, LORD, with all my heart;
> I will tell of all the marvelous things you have done.
> I will be filled with joy because of you.
> I will sing praises to your name, O Most High!
> *(Psalm 9:1-2).*

But to be honest with you, for the past month my heart has been far from this verse. In fact, everyday for almost a month I have told Billy, "I hate it here." "Have I told you today that I hate it here?" "Oh, and by the way, I hate it here."

While we were at the Dragon Hill Lodge I could easily imagine we were on an extended vacation. Everything was new and exciting even if extremely different and at times difficult. It still seemed like a surreal vacation. That changed once we received quarters (military housing). We were very excited to get housing! It took me only a few days to unpack the boxes and make the place look like home. But, it doesn't *feel* like home. I am a homebody. I could never have imagined a time that I didn't want to be in my own home. I need OUT! But, it's not that simple here. There are so many things you take for granted in our wonderful US of A! I miss home so terribly.

Does that sound like a "Happily Ever After" to you? No? Me, either.

~†~

I've just finished a Bible study by Beth Moore called "Believing God"' that is helping me to have a different perspective and to see my life in a whole new way. Beth talked about something I had never heard of although it's right there in the Bible, 1 Samuel 7:12.

Samuel then took a large stone and placed it between the towns of Mizpah and Jeshanah. He named it Ebenezer—"the stone of help"—for he said, "Up to this point the LORD has helped us!

Samuel was talking about Gilgal. It is a place where at least three times before Israel had suffered defeat and yet here they are again in victory! How cool is that? Our Bible study leader, Gail, as we discussed this particular lesson, shared with us about her struggles in her own marriage and how she and her husband had come near to divorce because of their struggles while he was stationed in Korea years earlier. Now here they are in Korea together and able to teach classes on marriage to others! That's a Gilgal! They have taken a painful experience in their life, seen how the Lord has helped them deal with the pain and struggles that must be involved in a marriage nearly ending, and they are now able to help others with their marriages. That's how it works!

I have striven to do the same. I have taken my Ebenezer Stone from one experience to the next, whether it's a past experience or a present one and I am learning to see how "the Lord has brought me thus far"! I've done this time and time again, sometimes in baby steps, sometimes in giant leaps of faith, until at last I find myself standing in my Gilgal. I have come full circle. I have taken the abuse and neglect, the negative thoughts and words, all of the hurtful, painful touches, and I am now able to use what I've learned from those things and who I have become because of them to help others. I am learning to take God's healing touch on my life to reach out to those of you who need to know that there is a God who loves and heals. And even if the God thing is still hard for you to believe, you can know that other people have been where you are and not just survived but thrived.

Yes, I still have battles. I still feel defeated at times and am tempted to give up, but most of the touches on my life now are positive and all I have to do is mentally see that Ebenezer Stone and KNOW that "Up to this point, the LORD has helped me"! I remember how far I've come. I realize how good I really have it in my "Happily Ever After." Even if the dishes aren't done, the kids' rooms are a mess, I am a continent and an ocean away from my family, and I have to stay here another two years so that my children can have some stability as my daughters near their high school graduation.

Look at things another way, Robyn. You have dirty dishes because you have so much food, and wonderful friends to come over and share it with you. You are far away from your family but you have a family! You have a God who delighted in placing you in a family that loved you and is proud of you! You have to stay in Korea for your children? Let it sink in that you have children, three delightful, wonderful children, and you are willing to sacrifice your desires for their well being and happiness. You didn't have that growing up. You didn't have any of what you have now or what your children have. Your husband is an amazing man who preaches God's word powerfully. He is real with his soldiers and he is faithful to you and committed whole-heartedly to his family. As if that wasn't enough, God gave you a lazy fat cat, a snuggly cute dog, a roof over your head, and plenty of friends who come in and out of the door, clothes on your back, books to read including His Word, plenty of opportunities to serve and a big screen TV that you can play Nintendo on when you need to de-stress.

I can't ask for a happier ever after than that.

Appendix

The Roman Road

This is for those of you who are yet to find God along the path you're on. Let me tell you about a road that may be able to help you in the right direction: the Roman Road. It's comprised of verses from the book of Romans in the Bible. These are some of the verses that went straight to my heart that day, nearly twenty years ago, when my college roomies decided to "practice" their soul winning skills on me...

For all have sinned; all fall short of God's glorious standard (Romans 3:23)

1. The first step along the path to your Heavenly Father, is realizing that you've messed up. We all have. God has high standards that we can't possibly reach on our own.

For the wages of sin is death but the free gift of God is eternal life through Christ Jesus our Lord (Romans 6:23).

2. As tough as the first step is, the next step is full of GRACE. God's grace in giving us what we could never earn or deserve. This is where we accept God's free gift of life!

So now, there is no condemnation for those who belong to Christ Jesus. For the power of His life-giving Spirit has freed you through Christ Jesus from the power of sin that leads to death (Romans 8:1, 2).

3. Once we accept God's free gift, He releases us from all the guilt, cleanses us of the stain, and gives us power over the sin that once reigned in our lives.

What can say about such wonderful things as these? If God is for us, who can ever be against us? Since God did not spare even His own Son, but gave Him up for us all, won't God, who gave us Christ, also give us everything else. Who dares accuse us whom God has chosen for His own? Will God? No! He is the one who has given us right standing with Himself. Who then will condemn us? Will Christ Jesus? No, for He is the one who died for us and was raised to life for us and is sitting in the place of highest honor next to God, pleading for us. Can anything ever separate us from Christ's love? Does it mean He no longer loves us if we have trouble or calamity, or are persecuted, or are hungry or cold or in danger or threatened with death? ... No, despite all these things, overwhelming victory is ours through Christ who loved us. And I am convinced that nothing can ever separate us from His love. Death can't, and life can't. The angels can't, and the demons can't. Our fears for today, our worries about tomorrow, and even the powers of hell can't keep God's love away (Romans 8:31-38).

4. What else is there to say? Nothing will ever separate you from Christ's love! Ever! Despite all that we've been through. His love was there. I know it's hard to see at times. Sometimes it's just plain impossible to believe that God's love was there in the crud of our lives. Read those last verses again. Can anything ever separate

us from Christ's love? No! Nothing. Just because there is junk in our lives, does that mean He no longer loves us? Again, No! Once you've truly realized that in your heart, there's just one more thing to do...

> *For if you confess with your mouth that Jesus is Lord and believe in your heart that God raised Him from the dead, you will be saved. For it is by believing in your heart that you are made right with God and it is by confessing with your mouth that you are saved (Romans 10:9, 10).*

You're standing before your Heavenly Father now and maybe there is something stopping you from running into His open arms. Maybe you are angry at how your life has been thus far. Maybe you have a mind and a heart full of questions and things that need to be said. Say them. Yell them. Cry them. He can take it. He is a big God, and I assure you, He can take it. He wants you to come to Him no matter the cost. Say whatever needs to be said but come to Him. Let Him wrap His arms around you. Let Him tell you how glad He is you've come. Let His tears mingle with yours as He tells you how sad He's been at your pain. He really has you know. He really has.

Acknowledgments

The author is grateful for permission to use lyrics and poems as noted here.

Pages 4-5 – "Beauty from Pain," as performed by Superchick, written by Max Hsu, Tricia Brock, Dave Ghazarian, and Brandon Estelle. www.superchiconline.com. Used by Permission.

Page 22 – Sara Groves, "The Word" copyright © 1999 Sara Groves Music (admin. By Music Services) All Rights Reserved. ASCAP. Used by Permission.

Page 43 – "For Those Tears I Died." Words and music by Marsha J. and Russ Stevens. © 1972 Bud John Songs, Inc. All Rights Reserved. Used by Permission.

Page 46 – Max Lucado, *When God Whispers Your Name* (Nashville: Thomas Nelson, 1999). All Rights Reserved. Used by Permission.

Page 47 – "You Can't Be a Beacon." Written by Marty Cooper. Copyright © 1990 Martin Cooper Music. L&G Music Productions, Inc. & Prima Donna Music.

Page 53 –"Treasures" by Martha Snell Nicholson, quoted in Charles R. Swindoll, *David, A Man of Passion & Destiny* (Nashville: Thomas Nelson, 1997), 67.

Page 75 – "He Touched Me" by Bill Gaither. (Alexandria, Ind., Gaither Music Co.) All Rights Reserved. Used by Permission.

Page 78 – Max Lucado, *He Still Moves Stones* (Nashville: Thomas Nelson, 2000). All Rights Reserved. Used by Permission.

Page 110 – "Housework" by Sheldon Harnick. Copyright © 1972, Free to Be Foundation. Used by Permission.

Page 112 – "I Shall Be Whiter than Snow" by James L. Nicholson. In public domain.

Page 124 – "I Have Been There" by Regie Glenn Hamm/Mark Schultz. Copyright © 2001 Designer Music/Minnie Partners Music. All Rights Reserved. Used by Permission.